# AMAZING ATLANTIC CANADIAN KIDS

# AMAZING ATLANTIC CANADIAN KIDS

### TEXT BY JOHN BOILEAU
### ILLUSTRATIONS BY JAMES BENTLEY

### FOREWORD BY MYRA FREEMAN

NIMBUS
PUBLISHING
— NIMBUS.CA —

Nimbus Publishing Limited
3660 Strawberry Hill Street, Halifax, NS, B3K 5A9
(902) 455-4286 nimbus.ca

Printed and bound in Canada
NB1410
Interior design: Peggy Issenman, Peggy & Co. Design
Cover design: Jenn Embree/Heather Bryan

Library and Archives Canada Cataloguing in Publication

Title: Amazing Atlantic Canadian kids : awesome stories of bravery and adventure /
words by John Boileau ; art by James Bentley ;
foreword by former Lieutenant-Governor of Nova Scotia, Myra Freeman.
Names: Boileau, John, author.
Description: Includes bibliographical references.
Identifiers: Canadiana 20190162694 | ISBN 9781771087971 (softcover)
Subjects: LCSH: Children—Atlantic Provinces—Biography—Juvenile literature. | LCSH:
Atlantic Provinces—Biography—Juvenile literature.
Classification: LCC FC2006 .B65 2019 | DDC 971.5009/9—dc23

Nimbus Publishing acknowledges the financial support for its publishing activities from the Government of Canada, the Canada Council for the Arts, and from the Province of Nova Scotia. We are pleased to work in partnership with the Province of Nova Scotia to develop and promote our creative industries for the benefit of all Nova Scotians.

# TABLE OF CONTENTS

FOR ALL KIDS
–AND THEIR PARENTS–
EVERYWHERE.

# FOREWORD

The acts of courage, bravery, and perseverance, as portrayed in *Amazing Atlantic Canadian Kids*, inspired historian, author, and researcher John Boileau to shine a spotlight on the strength of character and steadfast determination displayed by many young people when they are faced with extraordinarily challenging circumstances. We owe a debt of gratitude to Retired Army Colonel John Boileau for his contribution to the literary arts and for showcasing these remarkable stories.

Through remarkable examples of sheer will, this anthology brings public attention to the legacies of youth in Atlantic Canada, providing insightful lessons on character development, goodness, work ethic, and respect. Each person profiled in these pages cared more than others thought wise, risked more than others thought safe, and expected more than others thought possible. Readers will come away with an enhanced understanding that they, too, can overcome barriers with a strong will and hard work, give of themselves, and make a positive difference in someone else's life, all while contributing to the broader community.

Over my four decades as a public school teacher, a parent, and a mentor to numerous youth organizations, it has always been my priority to integrate critical thinking and problem-solving skills into a learning environment. I have seen youth respond to emergencies with split-second timing, demonstrating Herculean acts of physical strength and mental stamina. Often they were unaware they possessed these attributes until they were tested. Their capacity to find inner strength and take risks built self-confidence and served to motivate those around them.

This compilation of historical and contemporary real-life experiences honours boys and girls everywhere: those who risked their lives in big feats, who battled life-threatening illnesses, and who quietly performed selfless acts. These stories will encourage young people to seek out the hero within, speak up in challenging situations, or even just muster the courage to try something new.

It is my hope that *Amazing Atlantic Canadian Kids* sparks a conversation between readers, parents, and teachers about overcoming obstacles through tenacity and bravery. Perhaps it will also expand perceptions of what can be achieved, and remind parents and teachers that our young people's capabilities must not be underestimated.

Educating ourselves about stories of courageous individuals provides inspiration to each of us to make more meaningful decisions. By demonstrating courage ourselves, we can inspire future generations to do the same and make a positive impact on the world.

–The Honourable Myra A. Freeman, CM, ONS, MSM, CD
Former Lieutenant Governor of Nova Scotia

The Honourable Myra A. Freeman, CM, ONS, MSM, CD served as Lieutenant Governor of Nova Scotia from 2000 to 2006, with a focus on education, youth, heritage, and culture. Born and raised in Saint John, New Brunswick, she is a graduate of Dalhousie University. Her career as a teacher speaks to the emphasis she places on learning. Youth-related issues are a hallmark of her lifelong commitment to community service, encouraging young people to take an interest in the history of Canada, volunteerism, and public service.

Her pursuit of excellence has earned her many prestigious awards and honours, such as the Order of Canada, the Order of Nova Scotia, the Meritorious Service Medal for service as Honourary Captain (Navy), and six honourary doctorate degrees. Mrs. Freeman has also been named one of Canada's Top 100 Women, and was awarded the Progress Women of Excellence Lifetime Achievement Award in 2014.

# INTRODUCTION

All kids are amazing in some way, but some rise above their peers to do things that are truly remarkable. Such kids are the subject of this book: those from the four Atlantic provinces of Nova Scotia, New Brunswick, Prince Edward Island, and Newfoundland and Labrador, who accomplished something wonderful before they were sixteen. This includes kids from the past—the earliest was born in 1735—and the present day.

This list of amazing accomplishments includes tales of boys and girls who saved lives, received bravery awards, set sports records, invented something, established new homes in the wilderness, or fought back against illness, as well as many other surprising deeds.

Finding out about these kids and learning their stories required quite a bit of research.

I knew about some of the kids from my earlier books, such as Tommy Ricketts, who earned the Victoria Cross as a teenager, and the young heroes of the Halifax Explosion. Others I discovered by reading articles online or in newspapers; kids like Rachel Brouwer, who invented a simple water purification system for use in underdeveloped countries, and Olivia Gourley, who has already climbed Machu Picchu in Peru and intends to become the youngest person to trek across Antarctica to the South Pole.

Other stories required me to research the entire lists of the Atlantic Canadian recipients of the Carnegie Medal, the Star of Courage, and the Medal of Bravery to discover those who were under sixteen when they completed their heroic acts. In other cases, I became aware of amazing kids, like Olivia Mason who beat leukemia, through personal knowledge, or from the recommendations of friends, as I did with the story of early pioneer Robert Kent.

Some stories I even remembered from my own school days a long time ago. I recalled learning about Brook Watson, who lost a leg to a shark attack in 1749, and Anne of Green Gables and her creator, Lucy Maud Montgomery.

From these stories, it's clear kids should never be taken for granted, for they are capable of achieving great things. All that is needed is the right set of circumstances and the will to succeed.

# PART I
# REMARKABLE KIDS

> *What is the point of being alive if you don't at least try to do something remarkable?*
>
> – John Green,
> Bestselling American author

> *The first thing I have learned is you're never too small to make a difference.*
>
> – Greta Thunberg,
> Swedish climate activist

# CHILDREN OF MYTH & FICTION

Stories about children have been told since human beings first began to communicate with each other. Many of these accounts involved children in myths, legends, and fantasies. Some of them developed into fairy tales, like Hansel and Gretel or Little Red Riding Hood. Beginning in the late 1800s and early 1900s, stories with boys and girls as the main characters became a staple of children's literature. Iconic characters like Huckleberry Finn, Alice in Wonderland, Superboy and Supergirl, Harry Potter, and Katniss Everdeen have been read and enjoyed by millions of children around the world. Among Indigenous peoples, oral storytelling has a long and respected history of being an important way of entertaining people and sharing information.

Some of the children of myth and fiction are from Atlantic Canada.

# MAQ

Maq was a young Mi'kmaw boy who could not seem to do anything right. He mumbled and was clumsy. Some of the other children in his village made fun of him.

One fall day, Maq encountered an Elder carving a pipe from a piece of soft stone, called pipestone. The old man offered Maq a piece of it, which the young boy gladly accepted. The Elder then went on to explain why pipestone is important to the Mi'kmaq. When they use such a pipe, the smoke carries their prayers to the Creator.

Maq began to work the small stone and created a little person out of it. He was so proud of his accomplishment that he wanted to show his grandfather. Maq put his carving into a small leather pouch and headed off into the woods to walk to his grandfather's home.

While walking through the forest, Maq saw something moving in the trees ahead of him. It was a man, his long hair gently blowing in the breeze. When Maq told him that he was off to visit his grandfather, the man asked if he could join him.

As they walked together along the forest path, the man showed Maq where to find the best berries. When Maq opened his pouch to stash the berries, the man noticed the carving and asked what it was. Maq explained and the man said he thought Maq's grandfather would be impressed. The man then asked Maq his name, but instead of answering, Maq asked the man his. The man just chuckled.

The next day, Maq and the man journeyed through the forest, setting up camp at night and building a fire to keep warm. As they slept, Maq's tiny figure glowed in the dark.

On the second day, the two came to the edge of a large field. When the man said they had to cross it, Maq set off at a run. He skipped, hopped, and jumped his way gracefully across the field. He did not stumble or fall even once. When they were almost across the field, the man asked Maq his name again. In response, Maq asked the man his name. This time the man answered: Mi'kmuesu. Maq then told him his name: Maq—Mi'kmaq.

That night, they set up camp again. When Mi'kmuesu began to dance around the fire, Maq joined him. He felt strong.

The next day, the two travelling companions saw Maq's grand-father's village in the distance. Maq ran ahead and was greeted warmly by his grandfather. Before they went into the village, Maq brought out the little figure he had carved.

His grandfather was impressed and asked Maq why he had carved it. Maq replied he wanted to make something out of what he had been given. Maq said Mi'kmuesu had asked him the same thing. The grandfather reacted with surprise and asked the boy what he meant by "Mi'kmuesu."

Maq explained Mi'kmuesu was his new friend, and that they had spent the last three days travelling together. Maq's grandfather was confused. He told Maq the boy had been seen leaving his village only two hours earlier. Then Maq's grandfather leaned forward and whispered to Maq that Mi'kmuesu was a spirit who liked to play tricks on people, but who could also take human form, appear or disappear at will, and give supernatural powers to humans. He explained the tiny figure brought Maq good luck and he must keep it with him at all times to continue to be lucky in the future.

They went into the village together, where Maq told of his adventures with Mi'kmuesu, all without mumbling or stuttering. The villagers were amazed at the stories—and Maq's newfound ability to dance. Maq never forgot what his grandfather told him and kept the little carving with him always. Maq also now understood that he was unique with his own special talents and was less concerned about making a good impression on others.

Did Mi'kmuesu change Maq, or did Maq change himself after spending time with Mi'kmuesu?

What do you think?

# PEGGY

"It was a dark and stormy night."

We've all heard scary stories that start this way, but in this case it was true. It was, in fact, a dark and stormy night in October 1848. A schooner was sailing across the Atlantic Ocean from Hamburg, Germany, to the United States. Along with its sixty passengers, it also carried food and supplies for them to start their new lives in the New World.

That night a fierce storm blew up. Lighting flashed and thunder boomed as wind and waves made the vessel hard to control. With the frightened passengers huddling below deck, the schooner's captain tried his best to steer the ship into the relative safety of St. Margarets Bay, on Nova Scotia's south shore.

With a grinding crash, the wooden vessel slammed into Halibut Rock off Lighthouse Point at the southeast corner of the bay and quickly broke up into thousands of pieces. In the midst of the debris, a little blonde girl surfaced in the cold water, frantically looking for something to cling to. She grabbed a piece of wood, one big enough to keep her afloat. Driven by waves, the little girl was pushed toward shore, where huge breakers crashed against even bigger rocks. She knew if she hit them, she would not survive.

Luckily, the wind and waves did not drive her onto the rocky shore, but into a small sheltered cove. She drifted into the tiny inlet, clinging weakly to the piece of wreckage. Some of the villagers, who had heard the ship breaking up, watched the disaster unfold each time lightning lit up the scene, unable to help.

As the first streaks of dawn appeared in the sky, one of the onlookers spotted the girl in the cove. Several of them rushed down to the shore and pulled the soaking, shivering child from the icy water. Amazingly, she was alive—the only survivor of the shipwreck.

They wrapped the trembling girl in blankets and took her to the warmth of a nearby house. There, they gave her dry clothes and hot drinks. Soon, the exhausted little girl fell into a deep sleep. One of the men gently lifted her into a warm and cozy bed.

When she awoke the next day, the trauma of the shipwreck had caused the little girl to lose much of her memory. She did not know where she had come from or where she was going; the only thing she remembered was her name: Margaret.

As Margaret regained her strength, the villagers debated what to do. Eventually they decided she should stay in their small seaside community. One young man had a spare room and took her in. He started to call her Peggy, a nickname for Margaret.

Soon people from the surrounding area heard of Peggy and began to visit her. "Let's go over and visit Peggy at the cove," they would say. The visitors brought gifts of clothing and food and other things they thought she might need. As Peggy's remarkable story of strength and survival spread, more people came to visit. Eventually she grew up, married, and stayed in the cove.

Over the years, the village became known as Peggys Cove. With its picturesque lighthouse, the cove attracts thousands of visitors every year who take photographs of the lighthouse and learn the amazing story of the young girl who drifted ashore one dark and stormy night.

# ANNE

One of world literature's best-loved young characters, Anne Shirley—better known as Anne of Green Gables—was created on Prince Edward Island in 1908. *Anne of Green Gables* has sold more than fifty million copies and has been translated into more than forty languages. It is taught in many schools worldwide.

Anne is particularly popular in Japan, where she is known as "Red-Haired Anne." Lots of Japanese tourists travel all the way to Prince Edward Island every year just to visit locations from the book. There was even a theme park in Japan called Canadian World, which contained a full-size replica of the Green Gables house, but it closed in 2016.

The story opens with a middle-aged brother and sister, Matthew and Marilla Cuthbert, needing help running their farm, known as Green Gables. When the Cuthberts ask to adopt a boy from the local orphanage, the home sends a girl—Anne—by mistake.

Anne is an imaginative, talkative, whip-smart, red-haired, eleven-year-old orphan. Although she is eager to please, Marilla—a stern woman—says the girl must go back to the orphanage. Matthew, on the other hand, is a gentler person and takes quite a liking to Anne. Marilla soon relents and decides to let Anne stay.

Anne can be dramatic, but is very sensitive about her appearance, especially her red hair, pale skin with freckles, and skinny body. She also has a vivid imagination, which soon brightens up Green Gables. Anne quickly adapts to her new home and enjoys her new life in the tiny community of Avonlea.

Using her imagination and creativity, Anne gives "more interesting" names to locations in Avonlea, such as Haunted Wood, Lake of Shining Waters, White Way of Delight, Violet Vale, Willowmere, and Dryad's Bubble. She also has some misadventures. While attempting to dye her hair black, she accidentally dyes it green. And, when teased about the natural colour of her hair by her schoolmate Gilbert Blythe, Anne cracks a slate over his head in revenge.

When she is sixteen, Anne goes off to Charlottetown, along with several of her friends, to earn a teaching licence. Instead of completing the course in the normal two years, Anne gets her licence in one year and wins a scholarship that will allow her to go to university in Halifax.

Unfortunately, Matthew has a fatal heart attack and Anne gives up her scholarship to teach close to Green Gables so she can help Marilla, whose eyesight is failing, on weekends.

Gilbert Blythe eventually becomes Anne's love interest. Her admiration is confirmed when Gilbert gives up his teaching position at Avonlea School to work at another one, so Anne can teach in Avonlea and be close to Marilla. As a result of this kind act, the friendship between Anne and Gilbert is confirmed and the book ends with Anne looking forward to the future.

———◦◦◦———

You can visit the real Green Gables in Cavendish, PEI, during the summertime. There are guided tours, on-site museums, and you can even walk the Haunted Wood as described in the book. As well, a musical version of the story is performed each summer as part of the Charlottetown Festival.

Lucy Maud Montgomery (1874–1942) wrote six books about Anne Shirley and the village of Cavendish, Prince Edward Island (which she used as a model for Avonlea). The first book, *Anne of Green Gables*, follows Anne from ages eleven to sixteen. Montgomery also wrote lots other books, stories, poems, and articles in which Anne is not the main character.

Montgomery began her writing career when she was only fifteen, publishing a poem in PEI's main newspaper, the *Charlottetown Daily Patriot*, titled "The Legend of Cape Leforce." A few months later, she entered "The Wreck of the Marco Polo" in a prize essay competition sponsored by the *Montreal Witness* newspaper. It was published in the *Witness* in 1891 and reprinted in the *Patriot*.

The article was about one of the world's fastest and most famous clipper ships, the *Marco Polo*, which was launched in Saint John, New Brunswick, in 1851 and ran aground in a storm literally on Montgomery's front doorstep in 1883. She was only eight years old at the time, but the memory of that event stayed with her and played an important part in launching her literary career.

And what an amazing literary career Montgomery had. For example, since its publication in 1908, *Anne of Green Gables* has never been out of print. Besides the phenomenal success of the books, the story of Anne has been made into movies, TV shows, musicals, and plays—and has provided an endless array of Anne souvenirs.

# CHAPTER 2

# BOY SOLDIERS

**B**oys going to war as adult soldiers has been a practice in armies around the world for hundreds of years. In Atlantic Canada, boys first appeared as soldiers in the French colony of Acadia. They served in *troupes de la marine* or *compagnies franches* and were usually sons of officers. This made them members of an elite and set them apart from "ordinary" soldiers, who were largely from the lower classes. These boys served in an unofficial capacity in hopes of eventually being admitted into the *garde de marine*, which was the entry level for officers.

When Canada was founded and developed its own armed forces, this tradition continued, first in the Canadian Army, and then in the Royal Canadian Navy and the Royal Canadian Air Force once they were formed.

The term "boy soldier" usually refers to someone under the legal age of enrollment—normally eighteen—who somehow joins up, often by deceiving recruiting officers in some way. This could include lying about his age, presenting fake documents (or using those of an older relative), or even dressing in a way to appear older.

During the First World War, between fifteen and twenty thousand underage Canadians signed up to fight, and about two thousand of them were killed overseas. Some boys enrolled to escape unhappy homes or workplaces. Others joined for a regular job. Some wanted to avenge the death of a father or other relative killed overseas. Whatever their reasons, the vast majority of these boys served with pride and carried out their duties with distinction.

# THE YOUNGEST VC

Private Tommy Ricketts looked around and took stock of the situation. It was not good. Tommy and his small group of fellow Newfoundlanders were in an exposed and dangerous position. The operation had started well enough the previous evening, October 13, 1918, during the First World War, when the seventeen-year-old and his regiment crept forward under the cover of darkness. As they advanced, the soldiers came under German artillery fire.

Fortunately, casualties were few, and shortly after midnight the Newfoundlanders were in position: hunkered down next to the railway embankment, awaiting zero hour—the military term for the time an operation is to start—which was set for 5:35 A.M. Catching their breath in the cool damp air, the lads did not dwell on the notion that the next few hours could be their last. Instead, they resolved to carry on as best they could.

Tommy, however, would do a lot more than that. His heroic deeds would earn him the British Empire's highest military award— the Victoria Cross (VC).

⋙◦◦◦⋘

Tommy Ricketts came from a small fishing village near St. John's, Newfoundland. (Newfoundland did not become a province of Canada until 1949; before then it was a Dominion of the British Empire.) As a youngster, he was a member of the Church Lads' Brigade, an early cadet movement. In September 1916, Tommy lied about his age to get into the army and enrolled in the Newfoundland Regiment. Although he was only fifteen, he declared his age as eighteen years and three months.

Tommy went overseas to Britain in April of the next year and arrived in France in June 1917. On October 14, 1918, Tommy was in action in Belgium. During an early morning attack in heavy ground mist, the regiment, led on the right by Tommy's B Company, drove the Germans back and captured three of their pillboxes—small, partly underground, concrete structures. By mid-morning the mist had lifted, revealing the Wulfdambeek, a stream two metres deep that had to be crossed in full view of the enemy.

The regiment crossed, but suffered several dead and wounded. They had advanced another nine hundred metres when they were stopped by enemy shelling. The unit had gone farther forward than the shells from its artillery guns could reach and casualties began to mount.

Tommy's platoon commander, Lieutenant Stanley Newman, with a small group of men and a Lewis light machine gun detachment that included Tommy, went forward to try and move around the German gun position from the side. When they had advanced as far as they could, Tommy volunteered to go farther with his section commander, Lance Corporal Matthew Brazil, in another attempt to outflank the Germans.

The two soldiers advanced in quick rushes, under heavy enemy fire, until they were about 275 metres from the German battery.

Then they ran out of ammunition.

When the enemy soldiers realized this, they began bringing up reinforcements.

Volunteering again, Tommy dashed back ninety metres to his unit, picked up some ammunition, and returned to his section commander, all the time under heavy fire. With the additional ammunition, Tommy and Lance Corporal Brazil, the only two unwounded Newfoundlanders remaining in their small group, forced the Germans back to some nearby farm buildings.

As a result, Tommy's platoon advanced without losing any more men. When it was over, the Newfoundlanders had captured five field guns, four machine guns, and eight prisoners. For his heroism, Tommy was awarded the Victoria Cross. Later the French government presented him with the Croix de Guerre with Gold Star.

Tommy received his Victoria Cross on January 19, 1919, in England, at the country estate of King George V. The ceremony was a private one, as the King and Queen were in mourning for their youngest son, Prince John, who had died the day before. The King read aloud the citation for the award, which had been published in the *London Gazette* two weeks earlier, then pinned the medal on Tommy's chest. Turning to the small group in attendance, he remarked, "This is the youngest VC in my army."

The next day the King wrote in his diary: *Yesterday I gave the VC to Private Ricketts, Newfoundland Regiment, who is only 17½ now, a splendid boy.*

Tommy Ricketts is one of only eight people under the age of eighteen who have ever been awarded the Victoria Cross.

# THE VICTORIA CROSS

The Victoria Cross is probably the rarest award for gallantry in the world. It was instituted by Queen Victoria in 1856 to recognize the bravery of soldiers who had fought in the Crimean War, 1854–56. The first Canadian to receive the VC was Lieutenant Alexander Roberts Dunn in 1857. Canadians have earned 99 of the 1,358 British Empire/Commonwealth VCs ever awarded. Ten were awarded in British colonial wars (including 5 during the Boer War), 73 in the First World War, and 16 in the Second World War.

In 1993, the Canadian government instituted a Canadian version of the VC. While the British VC bears the English inscription "For Valour," because Canada is a bilingual country, the Canadian one was changed to the Latin "Pro Valore" to be acceptable to both English and French Canadians.

# THE BLACK BATTALION

When the First World War—or the Great War, as it was called at the time—broke out in 1914, black Nova Scotian men responded patriotically to the call to arms. Like all loyal citizens flocking to recruiting centres, they wanted to do their part for King and Country.

Despite being ready and willing to serve overseas—and contrary to official government policy—many black potential recruits were told it was "a white man's war." The vast majority of black men were turned away.

Amazing Atlantic Canadian Kids

Determined to serve, black Canadians and their supporters rallied for equality. They wrote letters of protest and approached local and federal politicians to make their voices heard. After two years of perseverance, the Canadian military responded.

This was partly due to the unforeseen high number of casualties on the Western Front in Europe and the need for more soldiers. Authorities decided on a segregated construction battalion, as they believed white soldiers would not want to fight alongside black soldiers, a reflection of the prevailing prejudice of the time.

On July 5, 1916, over six hundred black men came together at Pictou, Nova Scotia. This location was selected because it was close to the residence of Lieutenant Colonel Daniel Sutherland, who had volunteered to command the battalion if he could do so near his home.

Comprised of about 300 men from Nova Scotia, 30 or so from New Brunswick, another 70 from Ontario and western Canada, about 165 from the United States, and approximately 30 from the British West Indies, No. 2 Construction Battalion, Canadian Expeditionary Force was established. Its mission was to support the frontline troops on the Western Front in Europe.

All of the unit's officers were white with the exception of the Reverend William A. White, the battalion's chaplain. He was given the rank of Honorary Captain, making him the only black officer in the Canadian military during the First World War—and one of only a handful in the entire British Empire.

Thomas Goffigan was born in Hammonds Plains, Nova Scotia, and living in Halifax working as a shoeshiner when he enrolled in No. 2 Construction Battalion. At fifteen, he was one of the youngest members of the unit.

Regulations at the time stated that boys under eighteen years of age were not allowed to enlist—and had to be at least nineteen to be sent overseas. Even though Tom declared his true age and date of birth on his documents, he was still taken on. It's not that Tom was big for his age—a way many underage boys "fooled" the recruiters into letting them join up. He was only a little over five feet tall and weighed ninety-five pounds. Although the reason is unknown, it could have been that not as many men came forward to join No. 2 Construction Battalion as officials had hoped.

This was because of several factors.

Although black soldiers finally had their own unit, its segregated and non-combatant status undoubtedly disappointed some of them. As well, previous rejection on racial grounds may have dissuaded others from attempting to enroll again. Finally, according to a 2018 *Legion Magazine* video about the unit, several men felt the army let them join, "but wouldn't let us fight. They gave us shovels, not rifles."

Like many other boy soldiers and single men, Tom sent fifteen dollars a month from his pay to his mother, Emily, a widow who lived on Grafton Street in Halifax.

After training in the Nova Scotia towns of Pictou and Truro, Tom sailed from Halifax on the SS *Southland* with the Black Battalion—as the unit was often called—on March 25, 1917, and arrived at Liverpool, England, on April 7. There, the soldiers boarded a train for Seaford Camp on the south coast of England. After a short time in Seaford, Tom and No. 2 Construction Battalion crossed the English Channel to France.

There, they spent two depressing days in the pouring rain on a train followed by two more days on the road before they arrived in the Jura Mountains in the southeastern part of the country. Their camp, near the town of Lajoux, was to be home for Tom and his unit for the rest of the war.

At the camp, Tom and his comrades assisted four companies of the Canadian Forestry Corps in logging, milling, and shipping lumber—an essential commodity during the war. Lumber had many military uses: shoring up trenches, constructing platforms for artillery guns on soft ground, and making boxes for ammunition, among others. Tom and his mates also dug trenches, built railroads, repaired roads, and laid barbed wire. All of these jobs contributed to the achievement of the combat troops' mission in the front lines.

The tenacity of men and boys like Tom, who served their country while being treated as second-class citizens at home, is astonishing. They believed once they became members of the Canadian military, they might find some acceptance and equality but that was not the case. Even in uniform while serving overseas as part of No. 2, they were frequently subjected to the same prejudices they experienced at home.

Tom returned with his battalion to Halifax on the *Empress of Britain* in late January 1919 and was discharged on February 15. By then, he had grown almost four inches and gained more than twenty-eight pounds.

Although he had spent nineteen months in France, Tom was only seventeen years and five months old when he was released. Like all other Canadians who had been sent overseas, Tom was awarded the British War Medal and the Victory Medal in recognition of his valuable service to his country.

# NEWCOMERS

Humans have migrated to new locations since pre-historic times. In the earliest days, such journeys were often made to find fresh supplies of food or better hunting grounds. Some groups—known as nomads—spent their entire lives moving from one place to another, frequently timing their movement with the change of seasons. The Mi'kmaq of Atlantic Canada once lived this way, temporarily settling along the region's sea coasts from spring to fall to take advantage of abundant seafood as well as berries and nuts, before moving inland to the shelter of the forest when winter approached.

As civilization progressed, many countries sent out explorers to the so-called "unknown" areas of the world. It began with a search for a sea route around the north of the Canadian mainland. Such a passage was seen as a direct, short route from the trading centres of northern Europe to the fabled wealth—gold and gems, silks and spices—of "The Indies," which was the collective name for China, Japan, Indonesia, and India at the time.

Then, in 1604, French explorers and colonizers the Sieur de Monts and Samuel de Champlain and their companions set in motion a chain of events that started at Port Royal, Nova Scotia, which changed the world—and the lives of Atlantic Canada's Indigenous peoples—forever. These explorers settled the so-called "New World," in many cases pushing aside the original Indigenous inhabitants. These newcomers established settlements, which eventually formed colonies that later often became independent from their European homeland.

And the Indigenous peoples's ways of life—that had existed virtually unaltered for thousands of years—were changed forever.

<hr>

Still today, migration is sometimes forced upon people by war or conquest. They are driven from their homes by advancing armies, frequently with specific groups targeted for eviction. In other cases, people purposely leave the terrible conditions in their home countries to seek a better life in another country.

# LIFE IN THE WILDERNESS

Robert Kent settled with his family in the woods of Nova Scotia's Eastern Shore in the early 1810s. He wrote a rare first-hand account of his life and the hardships he experienced as a young child as he helped establish a homestead and lived in the wilderness. Robert's manuscript was copied and condensed by his grand-nephew in 1940, who read it before the Nova Scotia Historical Society in 1952.

Robert's experiences were probably no different than those of thousands of other early settlers in Atlantic Canada; what makes them fascinating is the fact we learn of them directly from him.

Robert's father, Lieutenant William Thomas Kent, served in

Britain's Royal Navy until 1813. After his release, he was appointed warden of the military prison on Melville Island in Halifax's Northwest Arm. The position included a house for William, his wife, and their daughter. Later in 1813, a son, Robert, was born there. Other children followed.

After five years, the Kent family moved to an island about forty kilometres east of Halifax, near the mouth of Musquodoboit Harbour. The island was almost connected with the mainland and consisted of about eight hundred hectares. It was known as Kent's Island for several years, but is now called Pleasant Point.

Robert's father built a log cabin where a tiny stream they named Smelt Brook ran into another body of water they called Oyster Pond. From there, a path ran down to the shore, where the tide run from the pond joined the harbour. Robert described it as "a pretty spot."

Today it is hard to imagine just how few people lived in Nova Scotia then. At the time, the entire colony only had about 81,350 inhabitants (compared to today's 940,600), while the population of Halifax was around 11,150 (compared to today's 415,000—almost half the inhabitants of the whole province). The small population meant the Kent family's nearest neighbour lived about a kilometre and a half away—and it happened to be Robert's grandfather on his mother's side. The next nearest neighbours lived about twice as far away, in the fishing village of Jeddore. It was a true wilderness: bears came out of the woods at night to catch fish, and the Mi'kmaq had seasonal camps in the area. There were no roads, just a narrow trail to Halifax, which was passable only on foot or horseback. All goods had to be transported over water.

Life as a settler family in the wilderness of Nova Scotia was hard. Robert's father was not an experienced fisherman, but thankfully food from nature was plentiful and close at hand. He also had a small pension, the result of wounds received during his Royal Navy service.

Though times were tough, Robert described some of the bounty: "There were oysters, eels, and lobsters, to be found in plenty, and there were wild geese, ducks, and rabbits. And sometimes a moose, to say nothing of a great variety of fish, both from salt and fresh water, some of which could be exchanged at Halifax for flour and other provisions."

While much of the family's food may have been readily available, not much else was. Modern conveniences were unknown to the Kents. They had no radio, television, telephone, or computer; no car, truck, or tractor; no trains, motorized boats, or airplanes. No electricity meant the only light came from candles or oil lanterns. As a result, daylight largely governed the daily routine: get up with the sun, and go to bed when it went down. Most people did not possess a wristwatch—and a wind-up clock was usually a treasured possession, if a family even had one.

Heat was provided by a wood-burning fireplace—and all the wood it burned had to be cut down and chopped up to fit in it. Water came from a well, a spring, or a stream, and it was drawn by hand, to be carried into the house in a wooden bucket. If hot water was needed, it had to be heated over a fire. The toilet was an outhouse in the backyard—chilly if you had to make a nighttime visit in winter!

Modern medicine was also unknown and doctors were largely unavailable to families who lived in the wilderness at this time. Many babies died at birth and many more children died young, usually from common diseases that have since been tamed by vaccines. Home remedies and folk medicines were relied upon, which normally depended on extracts from various plants.

As soon as they were able—and in any case at a very young age—children contributed to family labour. They would draw water; chop wood; maintain the fire; plant, weed, and harvest vegetables; gather wild fruits, berries, and nuts; fish; collect shellfish; trap rabbits…the list was unending.

There were no schools or churches for isolated settlers. Simple, at-home education was sometimes provided by parents, but it certainly was not a priority with so much work to do. A family Bible was usually the basis for religious education.

Robert's father bought a small boat and travelled to Halifax with his son, weather permitting. It took a day or two to make the trip there and back, a distance of about fifty kilometres by sea.

Robert often went into the woods with his father to help him chop down trees for firewood, carrying a little axe his father had given him. He recalled one morning, when he was about seven years old and wanted to help his father but was told it was too cold and he should stay home. He ignored his father's direction, snuck out near to where he was working, and started to chop.

It was going very well for him as he chopped around the base of the tree, but suddenly the wind caught the loosened tree and blew it over, pinning Robert's leg to the ground. He could not lift the tree or pull his leg out from under it. He began to yell for his father and, as he recorded later, he was thinking the whole time, "This is what happens to little boys who disobey their parents."

Robert's father eventually heard him and came to his rescue. He was able to lift the tree, pull Robert free, and carry him home. Although nothing was broken and there was no permanent damage, it was some time before Robert could walk again. But once he was able, he went back into the woods with his father.

Besides assisting with many tasks, Robert also helped earn much-needed income for his family. One day, he and his father gathered five barrels of spawning gaspereaux (also known as alewives—a type of herring) in Smelt Brook and sold them in Halifax for twelve pounds, "a lot of money in those days," as Robert noted.

When Robert was about eight, the family moved to a different place on Kent's Island, where his father built the first frame house in the area. He also bought a new boat, which he named *Britannia*, with the money he had saved.

Life in the wilderness was dangerous and Robert had a couple of close calls. On one occasion, he and his father were sailing from home to Halifax in *Britannia* when they were hit by a nor'easter. The violent storm swept everything from the deck, but fortunately spared father and son. Shortly after that, Robert was skating on Oyster Pond when he fell through the ice and got trapped under it. His younger brother could not get near enough to help him, but somehow Robert managed to get himself out. When he did, he promptly fainted. When he woke up, he was in bed at a neighbour's house. Not much later, he fell in again, "but this time got out without so much difficulty."

Robert continued to fish, trap, and hunt and became a very good shot. One day he killed nineteen geese (with only three shots), caught an otter in one of his traps, and collected five bushels of oysters—all before dinner. His father sold the geese for four dollars, the otter skin for eight, and the oysters for five. This money was important for the family's survival and bought items they could not grow, hunt, catch, or make themselves.

Robert's story as a boy ends here, but his narrative continued for many years. He remained on the island until he died in 1896 at age eighty-two. In the intervening years, the area's population grew. Eventually, Kent's Island had two churches, a large school, a post office, good roads, a bridge to the mainland, two lighthouses, and many small, prosperous farms. Almost all of its inhabitants were descendants of Robert's father, a man who, like so many other pioneers, settled the wilderness and established a good life for their families in the face of great hardship.

# THE LONG JOURNEY

The village of Ashouaihdate in Syria had a population of about four hundred. All the people there knew each other. Nestled between small hills and surrounded by a beautiful landscape of olive, pomegranate, and fig trees, it was a calm and peaceful place. Omar Maarouf, a farmer, and his wife, Khitam Damerji, lived there. They had three children: Mohammad, who was in grade six; his sister Chaymaa, in grade three; and his other sister, Baraaa, in grade one. Life in Ashouaihdate was good.

Then, in 2011, a cruel civil war changed everything.

Life in the village became very dangerous. There was fighting in the neighbourhood, with the sounds of rifle, mortar, and artillery fire echoing all around. Artillery shells fell on the family's home from time to time. There was not enough food and no electricity. The kids missed their school and their friends. The fear of death was always present. The family was scared and cried a lot.

The war had destroyed everything—not only their home and the children's chances for an education, but also their hopes and their future. Omar and Khitam knew their only choice was to leave or die. They choose to evacuate their family to a safe place.

First, Omar travelled to the neighbouring country of Lebanon to find work and make arrangements for the family to follow him. In the beginning, it was hard for him to find a job because some Lebanese people thought of Syrian refugees as people who took work from the Lebanese. Eventually, Omar found a job on a farm, where he would be able to rent a few small rooms for the family to live in once they arrived.

After Omar left, the situaltion in Ashouaihdate got worse. Khitam and the children—now increased to four with the birth of little Yousef—had to get out. There was only one problem: all the major roads were closed because of the fighting. For safety, the family banded together with some seven other families, who were also trying to escape. Fortunately, among them were two male relatives who helped Khitam and the kids.

Early on the morning of August 20, 2013, the refugees began their trek. At the time, Mohammad was eleven, Chaymaa nine, Baraaa six, and Yousef not yet six months old. Because the village was surrounded by soldiers, the families had to walk through orchards and valleys to access less dangerous roads and tracks. At one point, they got trapped in the same place for two hours because of shelling. Then Mohammad got sick and could not walk, so Khitam hired a donkey to carry him.

Life on the road for anyone trying to escape the fighting was risky. There were smugglers who wanted money to guide the refugees along less dangerous routes, but they could not always be trusted. It was a frightening experience: shelling, loud sounds, darkness, exhaustion, hunger, thirst, and stories of kidnapping and destruction everywhere. It was a long and harrowing journey.

Eventually, the families arrived at a main road and Khitam hired a man with a vehicle to take her and her children to Damascus, the capital of Syria. From there, they were able to get to Lebanon and reunite with Omar—a week after they had left Ashouaihdate.

Although they had escaped shelling and death, living conditions were not much better in Lebanon. The family was now separated from their relatives and friends and had lost everything—even some of their identification documents.

After three long years in Lebanon, the family received a call from an immigration organization—Canada would accept them! They were overjoyed. The family arrived in St. John's, Newfoundland and Labrador, on June 6, 2016. People welcomed them warmly and greeted them with smiles and hugs. The family felt they had discovered new relatives.

The Maarouf family was sponsored by the Muslim Association of Newfoundland and Labrador (MANAL), some members of which were immigrants who had arrived earlier from Syria themselves. When the Maaroufs arrived, MANAL had already rented an apartment for them (but now they live in a house). MANAL supported the family and helped them buy furniture, clothing, and o ther items, while another group, the Association for New Canadians, helped with finding schools and programs at community centres.

Omar was unable to find a job for two reasons: the language barrier, and the difference in farming methods between Syria and Newfoundland. Meanwhile, Khitam found work at a food truck that serves international foods. Omar and Khitam study English at a centre run by the Association for New Canadians and their fluency continues to improve.

The first month at Canadian school was overwhelming for the kids because language differences prevented them from expressing themselves or asking for what they needed. Fortunately, the schools were very supportive and provided English-language teachers. In addition to what they learned in the classroom, the children picked up English through after-school programs, friends, neighbours, TV, and social media.

According to Omar, Khitam, and their children, the most important thing for them is safety and peace—and St. John's, though much colder and wetter than Ashouaihdate, is a nice place to live safely. They feel Canada is a great country in which to live, with the potential for a good future. The family still has several relatives in Syria, Lebanon, and elsewhere, and they hope some can eventually join them in Canada.

Mohammad, Chaymaa, Baraaa, and Yousef love their new home, as well as their schools and teachers. They have made many new friends who have helped them settle in.

The kids also like the fresh air and the trees, which remind them of their home, and appreciate the beaches close to their house. Although it rarely snowed in Syria, the children always enjoyed it when it did. With snow all winter long in Newfoundland and Labrador, the kids are particularly delighted.

The kids' final assessment of Canada: a lovely place!

# PART II
# LIFESAVING KIDS

"*To save a life is a real and beautiful thing.*"

– Vincent van Gogh,
Dutch artist

"*I think a hero is any person really intent on making this a better place for all people.*"

– Maya Angelou,
American poet and civil rights activist

# CHAPTER 4

# BRAVE RESCUERS

The word "hero" was originally the name of a priestess to the Greek goddess of love, Aphrodite. Hero lived on the European side of the Hellespont, the ancient name for today's Dardanelles, which separates the part of Turkey in Europe from the part in Asia. Hero's lover, Leander, lived on the Asian side. Every night Leander swam across the strait to visit Hero, guided by a light in her tower. One stormy night, the light was extinguished and he drowned. In despair on seeing his body, Hero threw herself into the sea and also drowned.

Eventually, "hero" became a term to describe a person distinguished by courage or noble deeds. At one time, it was used exclusively to describe men, but today it has a wider use and is applied to anyone who achieves something outstanding. It is possible for anyone to be a hero—even youngsters—as ordinary boys and girls are sometimes caught up in events that lead to heroic acts.

# THE CRACKERJACK

HMS *Tribune*, a Royal Navy frigate, sailed from England on September 22, 1797, escorting a convoy to Canada. On board were 244 sailors and marines, plus an unknown number of wives (most with children) accompanying their husbands. On October 10, *Tribune* lost sight of the convoy, but carried on alone toward Halifax, Nova Scotia. As the ship approached the city's outer harbour on November 23, Captain Scory Barker suggested waiting for a pilot to guide them into the inner harbour. The ship's master, who was responsible for navigation, assured his captain there was no need for a pilot, as he had entered the harbour on several occasions previously. So assured, the captain went below.

*Tribune* sailed up the harbour, but began to approach Thrumcap Shoal off the southern end of McNabs Island. The master became worried, but before he could veer away, the vessel struck the shoal. The captain rushed on deck, sent up distress signals, and several craft set out to aid the stricken ship. One managed to reach *Tribune*, but the others were driven off by the wind.

The crew threw all heavy objects overboard in an attempt to lighten their ship and float it off the shoal. Even the ship's cannons—except one used for signalling—went into the water. It worked, and by nine o'clock that evening, *Tribune* was free. But it had lost its rudder and there were more than two metres of water in its hold. The crew immediately manned the pumps and seemed to make progress for a short time.

Then a violent gale blew from the southeast and carried *Tribune* toward the harbour's western shore. Four people managed to escape in the ship's lifeboat, but at about ten thirty the ship lurched over and sank off Herring Cove. Although Captain Barker and the remaining officers were believed to be lost, about 240 men, women, and children remained alive, either floating in the rough water or clinging to the ship's rigging that projected above the water. Eventually, about 100 survivors managed to climb into the rigging.

As the night wore on, the weather and water took its toll and many of those in the rigging could hold on no longer and fell into the water, only to be swept away by the waves. Soon, only eight survivors remained. Frustratingly, they were close enough to the shore to carry on conversations with the local inhabitants, who had lit a bonfire during the night, but the rough waves prevented anyone from landing.

At eight o'clock the next morning, a thirteen-year-old fisherman named Joe was the only person willing to attempt a rescue because of the rough seas. He rowed out in a small skiff and saved two people. Once the weather improved, other boats reached the wreck and brought off the remaining six.

Today, the location of the sinking in Herring Cove is known as Tribune Head, and is marked by a cairn, a bronze plaque, and the mass grave of the victims. The cairn also commemorates the bravery of young Joe, whose last name is unknown. As a result, the locals began calling him Joe Cracker. At the time, "cracker" was a British slang term for a keener or a go-getter. It perfectly describes the young hero who saved lives while adults stood by and did nothing.

# ISLAND OF DEATH

Teenager Ann Harvey lived with her family in a small fishing community on Isle aux Morts off the southwest coast of the colony of Newfoundland. Early one morning in July 1828, Ann awoke to a raging storm. She climbed to the top of a nearby hill and could barely make out the shape of a two-masted wooden sailing ship. It had been driven onto the rocks and was breaking up as waves smashed over it. Ann rushed back home and woke her father and younger brother, Tommy. The three of them, along with their big Newfoundland dog named Hairy Man, set off in a dory toward the doomed ship.

When they got as near to the ship as they dared, they sent Hairy Man through the huge waves to the ship. It was a Scottish brig called *Dispatch*, which had been carrying Irish immigrants from Londonderry to Quebec City. When the dog arrived, some sailors tied a rope around his middle and sent him back to the dory. Then Ann, her father, and her brother were able to rig a line from the ship to a strong pole on shore. This enabled the crew to make a breeches buoy, a canvas seat suspended from the rope to ferry stranded passengers over the water to land. In this way, Ann and her family rescued 163 passengers and crew, one by one, from the shipwreck.

The Governor of Newfoundland was so impressed by the Harveys' courage that he sent them one hundred gold coins and presented a special medal to them. In 1985, the Canadian Coast Guard vessel *Ann Harvey* was launched in Halifax. The ship is a search-and-rescue vessel and is capable of light icebreaker duties. Appropriately, *Ann Harvey* is assigned to the Coast Guard's Newfoundland region, with its home port at St. John's. Since 2007, the town of Isle aux Morts has held an annual four-day festival known as Ann Harvey Days to commemorate and celebrate Ann's heroic deeds.

# NEWFOUNDLAND DOGS

Newfoundlands—named after the part of North America where they originated—are large, strong dogs known for their intelligence and gentle nature. Male dogs, on average, are two-and-a-half feet tall and weigh 132–154 pounds, while female dogs are slightly smaller at two feet tall and between 99 and 121 pounds.

This breed also has a centuries-long record of service in rescuing people from drowning. Their webbed feet, water-resistant fur, and rudder-like tail make them natural swimmers. They also seem to possess an instinctive desire to rescue people in distress and have pulled hundreds of people from the water over the years.

# THE CARNEGIE MEDAL

Andrew Carnegie (1835–1919) was a Scottish-American industrialist who was one of the richest men in the world. He made his fortune in the American steel industry and during the last eighteen years of his life, he gave away about ninety percent of his fortune—some $350 million (nearly $80 billion in today's dollars)—to charities, universities, and foundations.

In 1904, Carnegie founded the Carnegie Hero Fund for the United States and Canada with $5 million to recognize heroic deeds. Annually, the Hero Fund awards the Carnegie Medal to people who voluntarily risk their lives while saving or attempting to save the lives of others. The fund also provides financial assistance to people who acquired a disability and to the dependants of those killed in saving or attempting to save others.

As of mid-2019, six Atlantic Canadian kids have received the Carnegie Medal. With salt or fresh water never far from most Atlantic Canadians, it is not surprising those they saved were all in danger of drowning. The details of two of these heroic rescues follow, with the four other recipients included in a chart on page 51.

⟶◦◦◦⟵

On June 30, 1923, ten-year-old Hugh Macdonald and three younger children were playing in a boat on a pond near Mira Gut on Cape Breton Island, Nova Scotia. When they were less than five metres from the bank, Hugh fell overboard.

Lincoln Tutty—who was only a year older than Hugh, and a poor swimmer to boot—was on shore and started to wade toward Hugh, but became frightened and turned back. When he turned around and saw Hugh struggling, he put his fear aside and waded back into the water.

Lincoln was almost within reach of Hugh when he suddenly stepped into deeper water and fell forward. Hugh grasped Lincoln's fingers tightly, but Lincoln freed himself, took hold of Hugh, and swam with him just over a metre to shallow water.

⟶◦◦◦⟵

On August 27, 1924, twenty-year-old Wenonah Shields was swimming in the Miramichi River at Chatham, New Brunswick, along with a number of her relatives. She had swum away from the shore and when she turned around to swim back, she could not make any headway against the strong current. Roland Roberts, her twenty-five-year-old brother-in-law from Moncton, who had earlier complained of feeling ill, attempted to save her.

He swam to Wenonah. When he reached her, he was able to support her for a minute, but then sank beneath the surface. Unfortunately, Roland Roberts drowned. Meanwhile, fourteen-year-old Frances Ullock ran from her house across the street, slipped off her shoes, and waded into the river wearing a long dress. She swam to Wenonah and reached her just after Roland had disappeared below the surface.

Frances took hold of Wenonah and towed her with great difficulty toward the bank. Part way there, a neighbour, Andrew Chapman, rowed out in a boat, picked them up, and took them the rest of the way to shore. Although Frances was tired and winded, both she and Wenonah recovered. Frances was also credited with saving the lives of three others in the group. In 1925, Chatham named its new ferry boat *The Frances Ullock*.

# OTHER ATLANTIC CANADIAN KIDS WHO RECEIVED THE CARNEGIE MEDAL

| Date | Name/Age | Location | Lifesaving Act |
|---|---|---|---|
| July 20, 1928 | Jane Clarke, twelve | Meduxnekeag River, Woodstock, NB | Saved Elizabeth Stevenson, thirteen, from drowning. |
| June 16, 1957 | Norma Horne, fifteen | Tidal creek near Alberton, PEI | Saved Ivan Richard, seven, from drowning. |
| August 1, 1965 | Murray Biggar, fourteen | Northumberland Strait, NS | Saved Patrick Dickson, eleven, from drowning. |
| July 27, 1985 | Darryl Pearcey, thirteen (also awarded the Medal of Bravery for the same act) | Southwest Pond, Holyrood, NL | Saved Cory Scott, ten, from drowning. |

# PLUS, A KID'S LIFE SAVED

It was sometime between 10 and 10:30 P.M. on Christmas Eve, 2001. Twenty-four-year-old Tobi Gabriel was driving her red Chevrolet Cavalier along Highway 209 in the area of Lower Cove, Nova Scotia. The highway there runs along the top of a steep cliff, unprotected by a guardrail in most places. Tobi and her three-year-old son, Gage, were on their way to join her mother in Moncton, New Brunswick, for Christmas. It was cold and dark, and it was hard to see that the road was covered in black ice in many spots.

Suddenly, the car hit a patch of black ice, skidded, and shot over the thirty-metre cliff. Although Gage was safely fastened into his car seat in the back of the car, Tobi was not wearing her seatbelt. The car hit a ledge, flipped twice, and landed upside down on the beach, not far from the water's edge. It was a complete wreck.

Tobi was flung from the car and onto the sand, where she lay unmoving close to the water's edge. Gage's car seat was also thrown from the car, but thanks to his seatbelt, the little boy was unhurt, except for a few bruises and a bump on his head. He began to cry.

About nine o'clock the next morning, Lower Cove resident Linda Belliveau looked out her window to see the Cavalier on its roof on the beach. When she opened the door to her house, she could hear someone crying very faintly. She rushed down to the shore. There, she found Gage kneeling in the sand close to the car. Although he was not crying very hard when Linda found him, she thought he may have been crying all night.

Gage was dressed in a winter sweater and fleece leggings, but had lost his shoes in the accident. Even though the temperature was relatively mild for December, it had been raining all night and Gage was wet and had small rocks tangled in his hair. According to Linda, the youngster "was soaked" and "cold to the bone." Gage's car seat was nearby, but no one knows for sure if he managed to unbuckle it himself or if the force of the accident tossed him out of it.

The Royal Canadian Mounted Police were contacted and, along with local residents, searched for Tobi. They found her body shortly afterwards. By then, Gage had been wrapped in a warm blanket and refused to let go of Linda until he was put into an ambulance. The only thing he asked for was a blue Popsicle, which Linda promised he would get at the hospital.

Gage was treated for his bruises, a bump on his head, and frostbite in his toes. He recovered completely. Gage told one of the RCMP officers two girls dressed in white—angels, he called them—had drifted above the surface of the water, smiled at him, and kept him company throughout the night.

Gage's grandfather believes those angels saved the little boy's life. "That's what kept him alive," he said. "If it wasn't for that, the boy would have died there in the rain." And as far as the residents of Lower Cove are concerned, they witnessed a miracle that Christmas morning.

After the accident, Linda Belliveau, who found Gage on the beach that chilly Christmas morning, kept in touch with the youngster. Gage went to live with his father in nearby Springhill, Nova Scotia, and grew up with him and his stepmother. When he graduated from high school, Gage joined the army and started basic training.

# CHAPTER 5

# EXPLOSION SAVIOURS

Whether caused by nature or humans, disasters come in many forms. Natural disasters include earthquakes, avalanches and landslides, floods, tsunamis, volcanic eruptions, blizzards, droughts, heat waves, hurricanes, tornadoes, and wildfires. Human-caused disasters are often related to transportation, industry, or the military. Some disasters can have both a natural and a human component, such as some droughts and floods. Atlantic Canada is no stranger to both kinds of disasters. Within recent years, hurricanes, blizzards, ice storms, and flooding have caused death and injury, as well as millions of dollars of property damage.

Disasters are scary. They are unpredictable—we do not know when they will occur—so it is often impossible to fully prepare, and their effects can be terrible: people killed or injured, houses and other property destroyed or damaged, roads blocked or made impassable.

Even if you have only experienced the loss of electricity for a few hours as the result of a storm, you know how helpless—and even afraid—it can make you feel.

# SPRINGHILL MINE EXPLOSION

Until 1923 in Nova Scotia, lads under the age of sixteen—known as "pit boys"—were able to work in underground coal mines. Boys were particularly useful in coal mines, where their small size made them ideally suited to some jobs. Boys also got paid less, which saved the mining companies money. By 1850, all the hauling of coal underground was done by fourteen- to seventeen-year-old boys, called "drivers." Each driver was in charge of a horse that hauled a coal-filled wagon on rails from the coalface to the mine shaft, where it was taken to the surface.

The drivers worked hand-in-hand with "trappers," boys who were often younger than ten. Since the mines were all underground, the airflow was controlled by a series of doors. Many of these doors were kept closed in order to direct air to a certain spot. Trappers, who worked in total darkness, pulled a cord to open these doors to let a driver and his horse through and then closed them again when the wagon had passed.

At one time, Saturdays were full working days just like any other. That was the reason miners were working in one of the coal mines in Springhill, Nova Scotia, on Saturday, February 21, 1891. Work had started at seven o'clock that morning and the miners had taken their lunch break from twelve until twelve-thirty.

They had only returned to work for about fifteen minutes when tragedy struck. Fine coal dust, which had accumulated in various locations throughout the mine and can ignite spontaneously, triggered a violent explosion deep under ground.

Like other mining operations in the province at the time, several boys worked in the Springhill mine. Among them were fifteen-year-old Dan Beaton and his younger brother, as well as seven-year-old Pete Robertson and Pete's fourteen-year-old brother Dannie. When Dan Beaton heard the explosion, he ran to the spot he knew his younger brother was working. He found the young lad burned, injured, and with his clothes on fire. Dan beat out the flames, hoisted his brother over his shoulder, and carried him out of the mine. He refused all offers of assistance and carried him all the way to their house, where he laid his younger sibling on the couch.

At the same time, Dannie Robertson was driving his horse, Jennie, hauling empty coal boxes. He was sitting on the front box when a terrific blast of flame knocked him backward. It blew out his lantern and killed Jennie instantly. After lying dumbfounded for a few minutes, Dannie was brought to his senses by the sound of crashing timbers and rock falls. He jumped up and discovered his clothes were on fire. Dannie tore off his blazing coat and vest, painfully burning his hands and arms in the process, and started groping through the darkness to find a way out of the pit.

He had only gone a short distance when he heard heartbreaking cries coming through the blackness. It was twelve-year-old Willie Ferris, huddled under the chair he normally sat on to do his job as a trapper. Willie was only burned slightly, but was frozen with fear.

Although another explosion could rock the mine at any moment, Dannie took the time to help Willie. Because of Dannie's burns on his arms he could not pick the boy up, but managed to carry him piggyback until they met a group of rescue men. Dannie gave Willie to them and was about to go back for his brother, Pete, whom he thought was still underground, when he was told Pete was safe. Dannie then walked out of the mine and went straight home so he would not worry his mother.

Altogether, the explosion killed 125 people and dozens more were injured. Thirty of the dead were pre-teen and teenage boys. It was the worst nineteenth-century mining disaster in Canada. Contemporary author Robert Morrow called Dannie the "Hero Boy," and wrote in his book, *Story of the Springhill Disaster*: "As the heroism of this brave boy is perhaps unparalleled in history, an effort should be made at once to reward his bravery in some suitable way."

Dannie was eventually rewarded with a gold cross, purchased with pennies collected by children from the surrounding area. Sir Charles Tupper, a native of nearby Amherst, who was Canadian High Commissioner in Britain at the time, presented Dannie with the cross. One side was inscribed *In Admiration of Danny Robertson's Bravery*.

Dannie's courageous act eerily foreshadowed his brother Pete's heroism twenty-five years later. In 1917, during the particularly tough battle of Passchendaele in the First World War, Pete voluntarily went into no man's land to rescue two wounded comrades. He carried one in safely, but was fatally wounded by an artillery shell as he attempted to bring in the second one. In recognition, he was awarded the Victoria Cross posthumously, which means after he died.

# SPRINGHILL'S HISTORY OF MINING DISASTERS

Springhill is no stranger to the tragedy of mining disasters. In 1891, its first one—and its worst—occurred in the coal mine's No. 1 and No. 2 Collieries. In addition to those killed, dozens were injured, with many of the victims ten- to thirteen-year-old boys.

In 1956, Springhill's second mining explosion occurred when several cars from a mine train that was hauling a load of fine coal dust to the surface of No. 4 Colliery broke loose. They derailed, hit a power line, and caused an arc to ignite the dust seventeen hundred metres below the surface. Heroic rescue operations resulted in eighty-eight miners being saved, but thirty-nine lives were lost.

Two years after that, in 1958, the most severe underground earthquake, or "bump," in North American mining history hit the No. 2 Colliery. Rescue operations continued for a week, with ninety-nine trapped miners saved and seventy-five killed.

The tragedy left a lasting impact on the town: some residents were injured, the mines were never re-opened, hundreds of men lost their jobs, and Springhill's economy was devastated.

You can visit the Springhill Miners' Museum to see unique artifacts from the miners—things like their lunch pails and helmets—pictures from the mine and town, and even tour a mine.

# EXPLOSION IN HALIFAX

At 09:04:35 on the cold, clear morning of December 6, 1917, the reality of the First World War was driven home to the residents of Halifax, Nova Scotia. Twenty minutes earlier, the French munitions freighter *Mont Blanc* and the Belgian relief ship *Imo* had collided in the narrowest part of Halifax Harbour.

Steel grating on steel caused sparks, igniting benzol stored on the French ship's deck. It seeped into the holds, where more than twenty-four hundred tonnes of munitions were crammed together. The two ships slowly drifted towards the shore, *Imo* towards Dartmouth and *Mont Blanc*, engulfed in flames, towards a wooden pier in Richmond, a neighbourhood in Halifax's north end.

Suddenly, *Mont Blanc*'s volatile mixture exploded, blowing pieces of the freighter high into the air and literally shredding the ship. *Imo* was blown out of the water and onto the Dartmouth shore. Haligonians had just experienced the largest human-made, non-nuclear explosion in history. The destruction was immense. The blast destroyed everything within eight hundred metres—including the massive Richmond sugar refinery and the drydock—and damaged buildings for twice that distance. Some sixteen hundred buildings were destroyed and another twelve thousand were damaged.

Within seconds, almost two thousand people (including five hundred children) were killed by falling buildings or from the force of the blast wave. Nine thousand people were injured, six thousand were suddenly homeless, and twenty thousand were without adequate shelter, all from a civilian and military population of about seventy thousand.

Stoves knocked over by the blast ignited shattered wooden houses. Soon blazes burned all over the city's north end. Relief efforts began immediately, first from local resources and then from farther away, including other parts of Canada and the United States.

At about 9:04 that morning, Agnes Foran, twelve, and her mother were looking out the window of their Merkel Street home in the north end of Halifax when suddenly—in Agnes's words—"the sky opened." The force of the explosion blew in the windows of Agnes's house and threw her and her mother to the floor.

Agnes was covered in blood. When she stood up, she discovered her mother had been blinded by flying glass. Agnes found some pieces of cloth, dipped them in water, and washed her mother's eyes.

She led her mother out of their house and into the street, before returning inside to rescue her baby brother. Agnes found him safe in his carriage and took him outside to join their mother. Agnes ran up and down the ruined streets in search of help. Unable to find any, she returned to her mother and brother and waited until her father made it home from his workplace about mid-morning.

Agnes was weak from loss of blood by this time and was on the edge of passing out. Her father put her on a chair and examined her. Agnes's clothes were drenched in blood and she was covered with cuts from the window glass. Her father was able to wave down a man with a car, who took the Foran family to the Victoria General Hospital. Because there were so many other victims, it took several hours before a doctor could examine Agnes.

When he did, he made an amazing discovery. A piece of glass about half the size of an adult hand had been driven into Agnes's stomach. Only a tiny point was visible through her skin. The glass had to be removed surgically, and it took twenty-nine stitches to close her wound. Fortunately, Agnes completely recovered.

───◦◦◦───

Before any outside help arrived, several residents—including other young boys and girls like Agnes—performed acts of heroism.

The explosion set on fire the apartment building where eight-year-old Norman Roberts and his family lived. Although Norman and his baby sister, Mabel, were not badly injured, their mother lay unconscious under a pile of broken furniture. Norman first tried to stop the fire by throwing burning objects out the window, but quickly realized it was of no use. He carried baby Mabel outside their shattered, burning apartment building and then returned for his mother. He was able to drag her out of the building to safety just before it was swallowed by flames. By the time she woke up, Norman had dragged his mother several blocks away from their home.

***

After nine-year-old Pearl Hartlen worked herself free from the wreckage of her family's flattened house, she discovered her mother was unconscious and trapped under the debris. She tried to pull her mother from the ruins, but her mother's skirt was caught on something in the wreckage and would not come loose. Pearl had nothing to cut the cloth with, so she bit and tore at the fabric until she could pull her mother out and drag her to safety.

***

Cecilia McGrath, an eleven-year-old pupil at St. Joseph's Catholic School, led eight other girls safely out of the ruins of the school. Another brave kid was Roland Theakson, fourteen, who calmly directed thirty-five small boys at the Bloomfield School—which had lost its roof and windows—to exit the building according the fire drill they had practiced.

# COLLISION COURSE

The Halifax Explosion should never have occurred. Even though the ships were squeezing through the tightest part of Halifax Harbour—appropriately called "the Narrows"—plenty of ships made safe passage there on a daily basis.

For reasons still unknown, the two ships—on a clear day on a smooth water surface—continued to bear down on each other, blowing a series of whistles signalling that each ship intended to stay where it was. When it became obvious the ships were going to collide, both captains tried to make a series of last-minute corrective actions to prevent it.

But by then it was too late. About twenty minutes after the ships crashed, a huge explosion snuffed out nearly two thousand lives, including those of five hundred children.

# CHAPTER 6

# NATIONAL HEROES

On May 1, 1972, the government of Canada instituted a new system of awards to recognize bravery. Three medals were created: the Cross of Valour (CV), the Star of Courage (SC), and the Medal of Bravery (MB). The first medals were awarded on July 20 of that year. Before the creation of these new medals, Canadians who performed acts of bravery had been eligible for various British medals. Generally, these medals were designated for either civilians or members of the armed forces, although some could be awarded to both civilians and military personnel.

In the new Canadian system, both civilians and members of the military became eligible for these medals. All the administrative requirements for the CV, SC, and MB are handled at Rideau Hall in Ottawa. As of mid-2019, 19 CVs, as well 461 SCs and 3,243 MBs have been awarded, a number of them posthumously.

Although no Atlantic Canadian kids have received the CV, as of mid-2019 five of them have been awarded the SC, while four have received the MB.

# MEDAL OF BRAVERY

The Medal of Bravery is Canada's third-highest award for bravery, after the Cross of Valour and the Star of Courage. The medal can be awarded to both living and deceased individuals, who have performed "acts of bravery in hazardous circumstances." Although recipients do not have to be Canadian and the act does not have to occur in Canada, the act must involve Canadians or Canadian interests. Anyone awarded the Medal of Bravery is entitled to use the letters MB after their name, which are known as post-nominals.

The details of two of these heroic rescues follow, with the two other MB recipients included in a chart on page 69.

# UNDER THE BRIDGE

Late on the afternoon of December 29, 1981, three children were on their way home from school and stopped to play on the ice under the Nasonworth Bridge outside Fredericton, New Brunswick.

One of the children, a six-year-old girl, had walked out onto the ice when it gave way and she fell into the freezing water. The girl's brother, eight-year-old Shawn Leckey, immediately ran to his sister's aid and crawled out onto the thin ice. He managed to grab her arms but was not strong enough to pull her out.

With the ice cracking all around them, eleven-year-old Chris Rector approached on his hands and knees and stretched out beside Shawn. Together, they were able to pull the little girl to safety.

Both boys received the Medal of Bravery on June 24, 1983.

# FIRE!

After helping his sick mother to bed on the evening of July 12, 1996, in Claredon, New Brunswick, eleven-year-old Tommy Coulombe went to his bedroom to play. He closed the door behind him so as not to disturb her sleep. Minutes later he heard a smoke alarm beeping and opened his door to be greeted by a wall of thick, black smoke.

Tommy ran to his mother's bedroom and desperately tried to wake her up, but she had taken medication and was deeply asleep. Without regard for his own safety, Tommy persisted until she woke up, dazed and coughing from the smoke. He helped her out of bed and remembered the fire safety drills he had practiced in school. He got his mother to crouch beneath the smoke and crawl.

Together, they escaped down a darkened hallway and made it out just before the entire house was engulfed in flames. Mother and son were taken to a hospital and treated for smoke inhalation.

Tommy received the Medal of Bravery on June 22, 2001.

## OTHER ATLANTIC CANADIAN KIDS WHO RECEIVED THE MEDAL OF BRAVERY

| Date | Name/Age | Location | Lifesaving Act |
|---|---|---|---|
| February 24, 1980 | Karen Jones, twelve | Moreton's Harbour, NL | Saved her brother, four, and another boy, two-and-a-half, from drowning. |
| July 14, 1994 | Jennifer Wilkes, twelve, and Amy Matthews, fifteen | New River Beach, NB | Saved Jennifer's sister, six, from drowning. |

# STAR OF COURAGE

The Star of Courage is the second-highest Canadian award for bravery, after the Cross of Valour. The medal can be awarded to both living and deceased individuals, who have performed "acts of conspicuous courage in circumstances of great peril." Although both the Star of Courage and the Medal of Bravery are awarded for heroic acts, the difference between them is the degree of danger faced by those who receive them. Those who are awarded the Star of Courage must confront greater hazards. As with the requirements for the Medal of Bravery, Star of Courage recipients do not have to be Canadian, and the act does not have to occur in Canada, but the act must involve Canadians or Canadian interests. Anyone awarded the Star of Courage is entitled to use the letters SC after their name.

The details of two of these heroic rescues follow, with the three other recipients included in a chart on page 73.

# HIGH DIVE

Courageous attempts to save the lives of others do not always succeed. On September 8, 1972, a young girl was attempting to climb down the side of a cliff to reach the entrance to a sea cave near Torbay, Newfoundland. Suddenly, she lost her footing and fell into the ocean. Fifteen-year-old Ed Duff of St. John's saw her fall and quickly removed his jacket. He dove twelve metres into the rough water in an attempt to save her.

Ed managed to bring the girl within reach of the rocks three times, but strong waves pulled them both back each time. Finally, he was totally exhausted from his efforts and could no longer support the girl's weight. She slipped beneath the waves. It was only with the help of others that Ed managed to get safely ashore himself.

Ed received the Star of Courage on August 2, 1973.

# HEROIC ATTEMPT

Sometimes heroes are very young. On the afternoon of August 20, 1984, nine-year-old Wade Nolan was crossing a rain-swollen stream with a younger friend at Conception Bay, Newfoundland. All at once, the smaller boy fell through a hole in the narrow wooden walkway and was dragged by the current into the mouth of Kelligrews Brook.

When Wade saw his friend being pulled toward an overflowing dam, he immediately jumped into the strong current to rescue the boy. The panic-stricken boy wrapped his arms tightly around Wade's neck. Sadly, both boys were pulled under the surface and both perished.

Wade was awarded a posthumous Star of Courage on December 5, 1986.

# OTHER ATLANTIC CANADIAN KIDS WHO RECEIVED THE STAR OF COURAGE

| Date | Name/Age | Location | Lifesaving Act |
|---|---|---|---|
| July 23, 1973 | Davie Critch, fourteen (posthumous) | St. Mary's Bay, NL | Died after saving his friend from drowning. |
| February 14, 1981 | Bill Ivany, fifteen | Sunnyside, NL | Saved a young girl from drowning. |
| August 22, 1983 | Kendall Isnor, thirteen | Kejimkujik National Park, NS | Saved a teenage boy from drowning. |

Amazing Atlantic Canadian Kids

# PLUS, A PROVINCIAL HERO

When Sherry Blinkhorn and her fifteen-year-old son, Daniel, went to sleep on June 23, 2009, they thought it would be like any other summer night. How wrong they were.

Some time after midnight, a fire broke out in their home in Barrington on Nova Scotia's South Shore. Early that morning Daniel woke up in typical teenage fashion to look for a snack. His first hint of trouble came when his bedroom light would not switch on. Then he noticed a smoky smell and had a bad taste in his mouth. He decided to get a drink of water from the kitchen to get rid of it. When he opened the door to his bedroom—which was next to his mother's—thick, choking smoke hit him and he could see flames licking up a nearby wall. Daniel's first thought was, *I'd better get out of here.*

He called out to his mother and heard her say she was already out of the house, so Daniel went straight outside and ran around the house. Once outside, he was unable to find his mother and realized she was still in the house.

Going back into the burning building through the back-patio door, Daniel crawled in the dark, smoke-filled halls to reach his mother's bedroom. He was relentless in hollering that she needed to get out, but was unable to reach her bedroom because of the smoke.

Daniel then knelt on the floor close to his mother's room and called her name over and over so she could follow the sound of his voice. Together, they both crawled outside, with Daniel shouting to keep his mother behind him. By now, both mother and son were almost overcome by the smoke and flames, but Daniel kept yelling for her.

Sherry Blinkhorn later told a newspaper reporter: "I'll never forget this as long as I live—I don't know how, but he kept saying, 'Follow the sound of my voice, Mom.'" Then she added, "I walked right through the flames when he grabbed me. It was that close." They only had time to take a nearby fire safe with personal documents before they escaped.

Sherry told the reporter she'd had a moment of anxiety over the thought that she might die and leave her son without his mother. She added: "There was nothing left of the home, but you can replace things. You can't replace people."

In 2007, the government of Nova Scotia created its own Medal of Bravery to recognize people who put themselves at risk to protect the life or property of others, with the first awards presented in 2008. Daniel was presented with his medal by the Premier of Nova Scotia at a ceremony in Province House in 2010. To date, Daniel is the youngest person to receive this award. Those familiar with the circumstances of Daniel's heroism made it clear someone twice his age might not have responded the way he did.

# PART III
# ACHIEVING KIDS

" *Believe you can and you're halfway there.* "

—Theodore Roosevelt,
President of the United States, 1901–09

" *To be yourself in a world that is constantly trying to make you something else is the greatest accomplishment.* "

—Ralph Waldo Emerson,
American poet

# GO-GETTERS

Occasionally, kids can face adversity because of the attitudes of others. People may act negatively or discriminate based on a difference—real or imagined—which they do not approve of. Such differences can be based on race, religion, gender, physical ability, economic status, dress, or sexual orientation, among others.

The kids in this chapter succeeded and excelled because of their raw talent and determination—proving wrong anyone who thought they could not achieve their goals.

# SHARK!

Brook Watson was born on February 7, 1735, in Plymouth on the southwest coast of England. In 1741, when he was only six years old, both his parents died, leaving him an orphan. He was sent overseas to live with his aunt and uncle in Boston, Massachusetts. At the time, Massachusetts was still a British colony since the American Revolution had not yet occurred.

Brook's uncle was a merchant. Before Brook was fourteen, his uncle signed him on as a crew member on one of his ships. One day in 1749, while on a trading mission to the Carribbean, Brook went swimming alone in Havana Harbor in Cuba, while nine of his fellow sailors were anchored near shore in a rowboat.

Suddenly, his mates noticed a large shark fin break the water about two hundred metres from the shore. It was bearing down on Brook, but there was not enough time to warn the young boy. The shark bit into Brook's right leg and dragged him under water. By now the seamen had rowed to the spot where Brook had gone under, hoping he would re-appear.

Two minutes went by.

Then Brook resurfaced nearly one hundred metres away. The sailors quickly rowed over to him, but by the time they got there the shark was attacking Brook again, dragging him under water.

One of the sailors picked up a harpoon and moved to the bow, hoping to spot the shark. After another two minutes, Brook re-appeared. The shark had torn off his right foot at the ankle. Blood gushed into the water from the boy's injuries. The shark moved in for a third attack, his jaws opening as he neared Brook. At the last possible moment, the sailor at the bow drove the harpoon into the shark's body, forcing it to turn away.

Brook's shipmates quickly hauled him aboard the rowboat and got him medical aid. As a result of the attack, a surgeon decided to amputate the fourteen-year-old's right leg below the knee. At the time, medicine was not very advanced and people often did not survive amputations. Combined with the other shark bites, the trauma of his near drowning, and the possibility of post-operative infection, Brook's chances of survival were estimated at 1 percent.

But survive he did, and Brook spent the next three months recuperating in a Cuban hospital. He is the first recorded survivor of a shark attack in history. Brook's missing limb was replaced with a wooden one—known as a peg leg—which, at the time, was the only type of artificial leg available.

By the time he returned to Boston, Brook's uncle was bankrupt and the young lad had to find other employment to survive. He took a job on a schooner owned by Captain John Huston that carried supplies to the British army at Fort Lawrence on the Isthmus of Chignecto.

Today the isthmus separates Nova Scotia from New Brunswick, but at the time it marked the disputed border between the British colony of Nova Scotia and the French colony of Acadia. The British had built Fort Lawrence in 1750 to offset the French Fort Beauséjour on the other side of the isthmus across the Missaguash River.

Captain Huston found Brook to be an honourable and honest boy, who was attentive and obliging. Brook was also willing to learn and improve himself, so much so that Huston treated him as a son, rather than an employee.

One day, some cattle owned by the English crossed the river at low tide and began to eat hay growing on the French side. No one noticed this until after high tide, and the English wondered if it would be possible to bring the cattle back. No one stepped forward to volunteer, until Brook said he would do it. He stripped off his clothes, swam to the other side, rounded up the animals, and began to drive them towards the river.

Suddenly, a number of Frenchmen appeared and asked him what he was doing on the lands of the King of France. Brook responded, "My present concern is neither with the King of France, nor about his land, but I mean to take care of the English cattle." With that, he returned with the livestock to the English side. This brazen feat was talked about by both the English and French, and certainly enhanced his reputation.

Brook's work was soon noticed by army officers and he became responsible for the management of all supplies for the British army stationed at Fort Lawrence—a position known as a "commissary." He eventually rose to become Commissary General of the British Army in North America and later Commissary General of the army serving on the continent of Europe. Because of his wooden leg, Brook was called "The Wooden-Legged Commissary" or the "One-Legged Commissary."

Brook returned to England and became a successful, wealthy merchant. He was an alderman, sheriff, and Member of Parliament for London, England. He also occupied the prestigious position of Lord Mayor of London, was Deputy Governor of the Bank of England, and was made a baronet of the United Kingdom.

Brook commissioned famous Anglo-American portrait artist John Singleton Copley to paint a picture titled *Watson and the Shark*. This dramatic painting of Brook being rescued by his shipmates caused an instant sensation when it was first exhibited at the Royal Academy in London, England, in 1778 and has remained popular through the years.

In his will, Brook left the painting to the Royal Hospital of Christ in London as "a most useful lesson to youth" who had suffered misfortune—such as being orphaned or losing a limb as he had—to show that even the worst adversities can be overcome.

# SWIMMER

"Get it done, do it fast, and just have fun with it." That's the personal motto of Danielle Dorris.

Unlike Brook Watson, Danielle, who was born in Fredericton, New Brunswick, did not lose a limb—she was born with only part of her arms, making them much shorter than average. But that did not stop her from playing soccer when she was quite young.

Danielle's introduction to swimming came when she was just three years old and her father enrolled her in lessons at the local pool in Moncton, New Brunswick. In the summer of 2008, when Danielle was five, her father, a major in the Canadian Army, was transferred from Moncton to El Paso, Texas. While she lived in Texas, Danielle continued to play soccer and also ran track.

In 2012 the family returned to Moncton. One day Danielle told her dad she was bored with only having one sport available in the summer and fall, and she wanted to try other sports. So, at ten years of age, she went back to swimming lessons. Because Danielle made such excellent progress, she was asked to swim competitively. Since then, she has broken both provincial and national swim records.

Danielle has a twin sister, Roxanne. In a news article from June 2016 on the Swim Canada website, Danielle claimed that Roxanne got "all the arts and singing and drama," while she "got more of the active side with sports and physical things." Being a military family, the Dorrises move frequently. Danielle feels having a twin helps her to get over the loss of friends each time they move.

Danielle is so fast in the water that she regularly beats her able-bodied teammates. Her coach, Ryan Allen, says she is probably in the top ten percent of her swimming club for kicking ability, which he believes is because of her powerful legs. This has allowed her to master one of the most difficult strokes in swimming: the butterfly, in which she set a new national record.

Danielle, now sixteen, says she is glad to have sports in her life and encourages others to be active. "So many kids go home and spend their evenings on their phone," she says. "It's good to have a sport," she adds, even if it's not a competitive one. "It clears my head; I'm not focussed on what's happened. Just what's in front of me."

Because of her speed and hard work, Danielle attended the Olympic and Para-swimming Trials in Toronto in April 2016. Her parents expected it to be more of a learning experience, and joked that she was only there to push the older swimmers to go faster. They felt if she did not make the team it would not be a big deal. But Danielle's amazing speed in the water did more than simply push the veteran swimmers, it earned her a coveted place on the team. Her coach noted initially there was no intention of sending Danielle to Toronto; their main focus at the time was on the 2020 Tokyo Paralympics.

At age thirteen, Danielle competed in the 2016 Rio de Janeiro Summer Paralympics in September, the youngest Canadian Paralympic swimmer ever. Because of the cost involved in going to Rio, J. D. Irving Limited offered financial support so Danielle's parents could attend and support their daughter. There, she competed in the 100-metre backstroke, 100-metre butterfly, and 200-metre individual medley, placing respectively fifteenth, tenth, and fifth.

Two years later, in August 2018, when she was fifteen, Danielle competed in the Pan Pacific Para Swimming Championships in Australia and won four medals. This included a bronze medal as part of the women's 4 × 100-metre medley team, another bronze in the women's 100-metre butterfly (where she broke the Canadian record during her preliminary heat with a time of 1:18:20), a third bronze in the women's 200-metre individual medley, and a silver in the women's 100-metre backstroke (breaking the previous Canadian record in 1:23:59).

Coach Allen says he always knew Danielle had potential, but never expected her to break two Canadian records in Australia. Although she went to the event simply hoping to gain experience and have fun, a two-week staging camp in Brisbane before the championship helped her to win the medals she did.

Danielle and her father both feel part of Danielle's success is owed to her relaxed attitude and her ability not to get stressed about competitions. "I just go with the flow," she maintains. "Honestly, that's who I am."

Her dad agrees. If Danielle does not post a good time, she tells herself, "Next time I'm going to do better."

"She's driven," her father adds, "but not worrying about it."

As Danielle stated in a CBC News article posted online in August 2018, she feels she and her fellow para-athletes "all have a special bond." In fact, she wishes "everyone was different because that's more fun."

Danielle has set her sights on swimming in other international competitions, especially the 2020 Tokyo Paralympics.

# PARALYMPICS

The Paralympic Games are a major international sporting event, involving athletes with a wide range of physical disabilities. Organized originally for a small number of wounded British veterans of the Second World War in 1948, they have since grown to include both winter and summer games.

Since 1988, the Paralympic Games have been held immediately after the Olympic Games. Additional sporting events for people with disabilities include the Special Olympics World Games for athletes with intellectual disabilities and the Deaflympics for athletes with hearing impairments.

# THE TRAILBLAZER

Born in Yarmouth, Nova Scotia, Aaron Cosgrove has lived in several Canadian cities, moving around with her family and her RCMP father. Four of her most memorable years were spent north of the Arctic Circle. The family spent two years in Tuktoyaktuk in the Northwest Territories, and two in Cambridge Bay (also called Iqaluktuuttiaq in the Inuinnaqtun dialect, meaning "good fishing place") in Nunavut. Among her memorable experiences were witnessing the brilliant northern lights, experiencing six months of total darkness, and seeing rare Arctic wildlife. Aaron believes these experiences fuelled her "hunger for adventure, world travel, and environmental and wildlife study."

When she was six, Aaron's family relocated to St. Stephen, New Brunswick, where she spent the majority of her young life. In middle school, she began to realize her "emotions and orientation" were not the same as most of her peers and became one of the first of her group to openly embrace her sexuality as a lesbian. As her "confidence and self-awareness blossomed," Aaron became involved in several organizations that combined her passions: Bully Blockers, a student-led anti-bullying club; Technical Crew, a club for students to practice their audio-visual skills; Youth for Youth, which sees teens helping homeless and at-risk youth in their community; Enviro-thon, a North-America-wide high school competition exploring environmental issues or challenges; and others. She even found time to play volleyball!

When she was fourteen, Aaron and a few other students launched the St. Stephen High School Gay–Straight Alliance in 2008. According to her first-hand account of her experience, described in a New Brunswick LGBTQ+ Inclusive Education Resource on "LGBTQ Role Models & Symbols," the alliance "took the school and community by storm in positive change and education." The group was later responsible for the passing of a provincial government policy that ensures the safety of and respect for LGBTQ+ students. Throughout high school, Aaron remained committed to the group through meetings, conferences, and awareness campaigns.

<figure>⸙ ◦◦◦ ⸙</figure>

Aaron graduated with honours and received the W. Garfield Weston Award for her "tireless work as an equal-rights activist in making St. Stephen a better home for LGBTQ individuals." This generous award completely funded her post-secondary education at the Nova Scotia Community College in Dartmouth in the Radio and Television Arts program.

After she graduated in 2014 with a Radio Performance and Studio Production major, Aaron worked at radio stations in Nova Scotia as an on-air host. She also volunteered with the organization Edge of Africa, in Kenya. There she studied and cared for rescued elephants, along with helping to operate sustainable community and conservation projects. All the while, Aaron has remained active within the LGBTQ+ community, never forgetting her activism start in St. Stephen.

# HOPE DOES BLOOM

In 2008, Jessie Jollymore, a dietician at the North End Community Health Centre in Halifax, had an idea. She thought it would be useful if local kids knew exactly where their food came from. Most of the clients Jessie was seeing could not afford the fresh fruits and vegetables many Canadians take for granted.

Jessie believes food is fundamental and impacts "every aspect of our mind, body, emotional and spiritual well-being." She had witnessed first-hand the effect a lack of fresh, healthy food had on families who did not have the means to purchase it. Sometimes people will lack energy, experience weight loss or gain, depression, dental problems, sickness, or even disease.

That was when she imagined a North End where children had a chance to break out of the cycle of poverty. Jessie thought it should start from the ground up—literally—with kids growing their own healthy food to feed their families and the community, perhaps eventually leading to a food-based business that would fund scholarships. The seed of an idea soon came to fruition and Hope Blooms was born in 2008.

That year, a diverse group of nine children aged as young as five planted their first vegetable seeds in an empty garden plot, close to where they all lived. At twelve, Mamadou Wade was the oldest. Tomatoes were the major crop and the youth gardeners harvested enough to make 150 bottles of salsa. Under the name "Salsamania," the kids sold their homemade salsa and donated the proceeds to a local women's shelter. Another idea was born: doing good in the community with the money they made.

The next year, 2009, the kids expanded their fledgling business. They grew more vegetables to take home to their families and also made preserves to sell at the Halifax Seaport Farmers' Market. They called this project "Super Sonic Vegetables."

In 2010, the project enlarged in two ways. Another six children joined, bringing the total to fifteen, and the kids started planting a few herbs, such as basil, oregano, sage, and chives. With the bounty, they made fresh herb salad dressings and provided samples at a few local markets. The next year they decided to produce the three most popular flavours and sell them at the Seaport Market. By now, nineteen children were involved and they had sold all 499 bottles of dressing they had prepared. The proceeds were used to fund a scholarship for a youth from their community.

In 2013, the Hope Blooms kids landed a coveted spot on CBC's hit reality TV show *Dragon's Den*. This program features inventors and entrepreneurs who believe they have a good idea or product—but not enough money—to launch a successful business. They "pitch" their vision to a panel of savvy investors (known as "Dragons") in an attempt to get financial backing, usually in return for ownership of a portion of the business.

After lots of practice with a pitch they wrote together, Mamadou led the nervous team into the Dragon's Den—and onto national television on November 14, 2013. There were six kids aged eleven to fifteen, looking for $10,000 to build a new greenhouse so they could grow vegetables and herbs all year long. In return for the investment, the kids offered a five percent royalty on future profits.

Mamadou started off the pitch this way: "There is a saying that it takes a village to raise a child, Dragons. But sometimes, it might just take the children to raise a village." Later in the pitch, one of the kids noted the motto of Hope Blooms is, "When you change the way you look at things, the things you look at change." The group also displayed samples of their three flavours of salad dressings. The adults who had accompanied the kids to Toronto then came out with fresh veggies so the Dragons could sample the dressings.

The Dragons were visibly impressed; a couple of the normally hard-nosed entrepreneurs were even moved to tears when they heard the amazing success story of Hope Blooms. At the time, the enterprise was thirty youths strong, had expanded to twenty-seven garden plots, and had sold $26,600 worth of salad dressing, on which they made $12,000 profit. Of that amount, the kids had set aside $4,000 for a scholarship.

Four of the five Dragons felt so strongly about Hope Blooms that they offered $10,000 each, without requiring any payback. The kids were blown away. Later that year, one of the Dragons (Jim Treliving, chairman and owner of the Boston Pizza chain) travelled to Halifax to present Hope Blooms with a cheque for $40,000—and to see the gardens for himself. With the money to buy materials, the Canadian Armed Forces helped Hope Blooms build its first greenhouse.

In 2014, Hope Blooms expanded to forty kids and started offering family cooking classes and community kitchens. That year they grew over three thousand pounds of organic vegetables and fruits—a new record. The organization also became a registered charity. The following year, 2015, Build Right Nova Scotia helped the kids build a solar-powered greenhouse next to the gardens.

Mamadou graduated from high school in 2016 and was accepted at the University of Toronto to study commerce. He was the first recipient of an $8,000 Hope Blooms Scholarship, and he also received a $70,000 TD Community Leadership scholarship. Mamadou is the first member of his family to pursue post-secondary education. Three more Hope Blooms kids followed Mamadou in 2017 and graduated from high school. They each received a yearly renewable scholarship for post-secondary education.

Meanwhile, Hope Blooms had grown to more than fifty kids, and Loblaws stores across Nova Scotia began to stock the group's herb salad dressings. By this time, Hope Blooms was producing more than four thousand pounds of organic vegetables and fruit, distributed for free throughout their community.

2018 was a busy year for Hope Blooms. Another high school graduate was accepted into St. Francis Xavier University in Antigonish. The group also introduced a new line of products: Possibili-teas. Proceeds from sales of the herbal tea blends are donated to single mothers in the West African country of Senegal. Mamadou, assisted by Jessie Jollymore and the youth of Hope Blooms, wrote a book called *Hope Blooms: Plant a Seed, Harvest a Dream*, which was published by Nimbus that same year.

Hope Blooms's impact on Halifax's North End has been tremendous. The kids have grown and distributed well over twenty thousand pounds of organic vegetables and fruit. Every single month they provide 206 healthy meals and 306 healthy snacks to members of their community who struggle to access nutritious food. They also started a farm exchange program in the Annapolis Valley, one of the most productive vegetable- and fruit-growing areas of Canada. Through this exchange, they've brought hundreds of pounds of organic produce to the city and donated it to 110 Syrian refugees living in Halifax's North End. In addition, Hope Blooms gave fifteen free garden plots to Syrian families so they could grow and harvest their own produce. The group continues to host food-literacy and cooking-skills workshops and community suppers, and also provides free soup deliveries to local seniors.

Through the amazing work ethic and commitment of Mamadou Wade and dozens of other young Haligonians, hope does indeed bloom in North End Halifax.

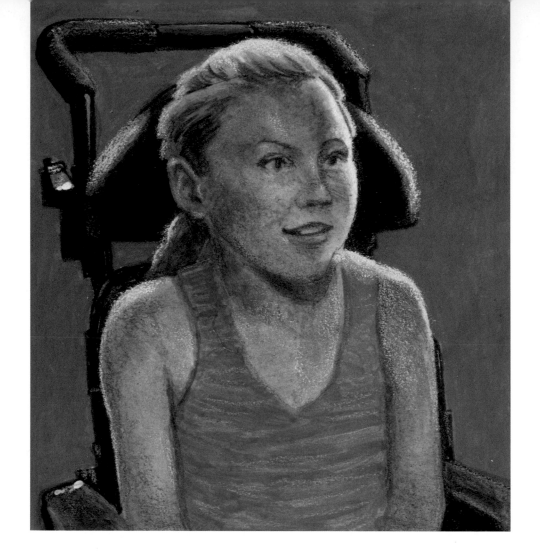

# THE QUICK-THINKING HERO

Lexie Comeau-Drisdelle was preparing to celebrate her ninth birthday on May 5, 2018, in Dartmouth, Nova Scotia. While her mother, Kelly, got ready for the party upstairs and her grandmother, Nancy, was in the kitchen, Lexie was downstairs waiting for guests to arrive and watching her eighteen-month-old brother, Leeland, playing in the dining room.

Then, to Lexie's horror, Leeland opened the sliding glass door to the back deck and pool, stepped out, and closed the door behind him. It was something he had never done before. Then he jumped into the swimming pool.

Lexie knew she had to do something, but there was a big problem: Lexie cannot walk or talk. She has cerebral palsy, a condition that affects her muscle movement and coordination, and she uses a wheelchair. So, Lexie did the only thing she could: she screamed as loud as possible. Lexie's mother thought her daughter must have fallen and rushed downstairs, while Lexie's grandmother ran to her from the kitchen.

Lexie was pointing to the sliding door. Her grandmother looked out, but could not see Leeland. It was only when she went outside that she saw him right at the edge of the pool and quickly scooped him out. Apart from coughing up some water, Leeland seemed fine. As a precaution they took him to the hospital, just to make sure he was all right.

For her quick-thinking actions that saved her brother's life, Lexie received special commendations from the Halifax Regional Municipality and Halifax Regional Police. As Halifax's mayor, Mike Savage, noted when he presented Lexie with her commendation, "Heroes come in all sizes."

# CHAPTER 8

# FIGHTERS

Kids are not immune from becoming ill, sometimes with life-threatening diseases. Fighting back against such illnesses requires tremendous physical and mental effort on their part. This can include enduring several treatments, lengthy hospital stays, reduced immunity, and weight loss, among other things. Unfortunately, sometimes, their best efforts are in vain. Whether or not they survived their illness, the amazing kids in this chapter have made the world better than they found it, and have left behind a legacy.

# THE WILL TO LIVE

During her school's winter break in February 2011, eleven-year-old Olivia Mason of Bedford, Nova Scotia, was on a skiing holiday at the Sunday River resort in Maine with her mother, father, and older brother, Matthew. Not long into the holiday, she began to feel a little sick and became exhausted casily. After every few seconds of skiing, she would have to sit down to catch her breath. Olivia recalls one time when she accidentally skied off a trail and went down the side of a small hill. It took her almost ten minutes to climb back up to the trail because she had no energy or strength.

When Olivia's parents, Tammy and Barry, noticed she was not skiing very well, they told her she probably needed to eat more. Describing everything later to the author, Olivia said that at about the same time, she started to get "a really bad pain" in the lower part of her body. Her parents took her to a local clinic, where medical staff thought she had likely picked up an infection from a hot tub. They prescribed medicine, but it did not help.

For the second week of the family holiday, the Masons drove from Sunday River to Boston and flew to a resort in San Juan, Puerto Rico. Olivia's parents thought she had probably caught a cold and maybe a couple of days in the sun would cure it.

But Olivia did not get better in Puerto Rico. She stayed up late, had a hard time falling asleep, and cannot even remember the mornings. She hardly left their room. Her parents began to get worried.

Olivia found her own lack of energy very strange. She was a self-described "high-energy kid," who was always "running around, making a mess, dragging my parents to after-school activities." When a burning pain started to shoot down her back, Olivia remembers lying in bed at the Peurto Rican resort, crying while her parents tried to get her to eat something. She could not walk very far without having to sit down.

Olivia's parents could see she was getting worse. They realized it was more than a cold and first thought it might be mononucleosis (commonly called "mono"), which her father had as a kid. But as her pain became worse, they knew it must be something else—mono is not painful and does not prevent someone from walking.

Her mom then thought it might be psoriatic arthritis (stiffness of the joints that affects people who have a skin condition known as psoriasis), which she herself had been diagnosed with when she was twenty-four. Many of Olivia's symptoms were similar. As her parents debated taking Olivia to a doctor while in Puerto Rico—who might not have spoken English—Olivia's appetite continued to decline. She remembers snacking a bit, perhaps a cheese stick and a little water, but "never a full meal."

When it came time to leave the island, the family flew out of San Juan to Orlando, Florida, where they had to change planes. In the Florida airport, Olivia was not able to walk at all and had to sit in a wheelchair. Her parents wondered if they should cancel the flight to Boston and just take Olivia to a hospital in Orlando. In retrospect, Olivia's mom feels bad they did not "ditch the flight," but at the time nothing serious had entered their minds. They were still thinking Olivia had psoriatic arthritis. The family flew to Boston and re-evaluated there.

⟶◦◦◦⟵

By the time they landed in Boston, Olivia's family realized her condition was worse than they originally thought. They discussed their options: a Boston hospital, or Halifax's IWK children's hospital. At that stage, they still thought all a doctor would tell them in Boston was that it was a virus or perhaps arthritis and a couple of days in hospital would fix her up. As far as Olivia was concerned, she just wanted to go home to see her dogs—and not go to a hospital in Boston.

So the family drove home to Halifax. Her parents knew Olivia was in pain, but thought they could make her comfortable lying out on the back seat of the car, with her mother rubbing her back. The plan was to drive right through to Halifax, but then they ran into a snowstorm and had to stop for the night in a motel somewhere between Boston and New Brunswick. No one in the family can even remember where it was.

They were on the road by six o'clock the next morning and made it to Bedford, Nova Scotia, at about nine o'clock that night. After dropping Olivia's brother at his aunt's, they drove straight to the IWK. Olivia remembers "wailing" that she wanted to see her dogs and being angry with her parents for going straight to the hospital. After only a few minutes' wait at the hospital, a nurse said Olivia did not look good and was "way too pale." She was admitted to an emergency room, had blood taken, and was put on an intravenous (IV) drip (a way of delivering medication into a vein through a needle). The results came back perhaps about thirty minutes later. They stunned the family: "Olivia has leukemia; we're admitting her."

Olivia's mom remembers saying, "No, you need to do more tests. I want another opinion. You don't understand, it can't be, last week this girl was on a ski hill."

Leukemia is a cancer of the body's blood-forming tissues, and the diagnosis was particularly upsetting for the family, as Olivia's uncle (her dad's brother) had just died of cancer two and a half months earlier. A cancer specialist (called an oncologist) came in and said, "This is your second opinion." Olivia had leukemia.

She was admitted to a sixth-floor room about midnight. Since it was early Sunday morning, the specialist said they would have to wait until Monday for further tests to determine what kind of leukemia it was. Monday's tests showed it was acute myelogenous leukemia (AML), a type of blood cancer in which the bone marrow makes a large number of abnormal white blood cells.

While all this was going on, Olivia woke up to find she had wet the bed, which upset her very much. "After all," she said, "I was eleven!" She was given a painkiller and started a blood transfusion.

On Tuesday morning, doctors tested the bottom of her feet for feeling, but by now Olivia could not even move her legs. This was followed by an emergency MRI that showed a solid tumour on her spine. Because of the location of the tumour, it was too dangerous to operate; one wrong move and Olivia could be paralyzed for life. So the doctors met with Olivia's parents to discuss radiation, rather than surgery, as a way to shrink the tumour.

Olivia had three rounds of radiation for the tumour and then started chemotherapy—known as "chemo" for short—for the leukemia that Friday. (Chemotherapy is a term that refers to one or more drugs used for cancer treatment, usually given through an IV drip.)

Olivia had to have a small surgical procedure to insert a device called a Hickman tube into her chest so she could receive chemo. According to Olivia, this is when she "started freaking out," as she had not realized until then just how ill she really was. The chemo treatments lasted five days and—as usually happens with chemo patients—the drugs made Olivia sick immediately and she could not eat.

Olivia had five cycles of chemo. Each cycle lasted twenty-eight days before the next one began. The aim of the treatments was to clear her blood of the immature cells. Fortunately, Olivia started to improve with round one and the following rounds were intended to keep her that way. It all took exactly six months.

After the second round of chemo, Olivia's mom thought perhaps her daughter would not lose her hair as most chemo patients do. But when Olivia woke up one morning and found a wad of hair on her pillow, she remembered that she "wasn't concerned about losing it." Hospital staff brought her a selection of wigs and hats, but Olivia simply "wasn't interested." In addition to losing her hair, Olivia also lost a lot of weight due to her lack of appetite. When she was admitted, she weighed around ninety-nine pounds. After the second round of chemotherapy, she weighed just sixty-four pounds. Whenever she got hungry, she knew her good blood cell count was up.

Olivia was in grade six during her health scare, and passed the school year based on her marks to February. She was released from the hospital in time for the next school year, but needed a cane to help her walk, and was unable to carry books or a backpack for a while.

After she was released, Olivia became a spokesperson for the Leukemia & Lymphoma Society of Canada, travelling around to schools to talk about her experience, and fundraising. She also made a video for the society, took part in the 2016 Light the Night Walk through Halifax, and was chosen as one of the society's Honoured Heroes. In grade nine, she was her class valedictorian at Bedford Academy, and even spoke at the Sackville High School dance marathon in support of the IWK.

After being cured, Olivia became a counsellor for children diagnosed with similar diseases and visited them in hospitals to encourage them. She also spoke at schools to let children know what to expect if they were hospitalized. Olivia's mom said her daughter's sickness gave her a new appreciation for the importance of family, especially the strength and support its members provide. For her part, Olivia noted, "I felt very lucky; I realize how unimportant we all are in the big picture."

In recognition for all the work she has done helping relieve the fears of children who are about to be hospitalized, and for her support of those going through treatment, Olivia was awarded the Queen Elizabeth II Diamond Jubilee Medal by Lieutenant Governor Brigadier General The Honourable J. J. Grant at Government House in Halifax on February 1, 2013.

# QUEEN ELIZABETH II
# DIAMOND JUBILEE MEDAL

The Diamond Jubilee Medal was created in 2012 to mark the sixtieth anniversary of Her Majesty Queen Elizabeth II taking the throne as Queen of Canada. It was awarded to Canadians from all walks of life to honour their significant contributions and achievements to the country. During the Diamond Jubilee year, sixty thousand deserving Canadians were recognized with the medal.

Olivia Mason was not the only kid to receive a Diamond Jubilee Medal. In fact, the youngest person in Canada to be awarded the medal was nine-year-old Bryden Hutt of Yarmouth, Nova Scotia.

Bryden has a disorder that left him without an immune system as a baby. When he was five, the Children's Wish Foundation granted him a wish –to go to Disney World with his bone marrow transplant donor. Since then, Bryden has been volunteering his time to raise money for the foundation. When he received his medal in February 2012, he had raised about $30,000 and has gone on to raise even more.

# #BECCATOLDMETO

Becca Schofield, a teen from Riverview, New Brunswick, enjoyed the same things as many other teenagers. She loved hanging out with her family and friends, spending summers at the family cottage, reading books and watching movies, trying out new foods, baking cookies, listening to music, playing games, and ringette. A naturally inquisitive person, Becca's curiosity got her into a few predicaments. There was the time a hot dog ended up in her nose, the time she had a close call with an electrical outlet and a fork, the quick visit she had to take to the hospital after sampling her grandmother's medication, and many more.

Becca was diagnosed with cancer in the form of a brain tumour in February 2015, when she was fifteen years old. Surgeons were able to remove the tumour successfully; that was followed by months of chemotherapy and radiation treatments to make sure it didn't grow back. Becca and her family were told she was "in the clear."

Then, in December 2016, doctors discovered two new tumours. They were inoperable, which usually means they are too near a delicate part of the brain to remove safely.

The cancer was back—and it was terminal. Becca was given three to twelve months to live.

One of the first things Becca did after receiving this diagnosis was to write a public post on Facebook. Even in the face of such devastating news, she kept her natural sense of good humour and named her two new tumours Snape and Umbridge after her least-favourite Harry Potter characters. Among other things, Becca went on to note that although she was sad she would never get married, she was happy she would stop being sick. She had mixed emotions over never graduating from high school, but was happy to be done with math.

That same month, Becca gained national attention when she posted another Facebook message that went viral. In it, she asked people to perform acts of kindness and share them on social media with the hashtag #BeccaToldMeTo. "No matter who you are, if you see this message, please do an act of kindness for someone else," she wrote. "It can be as big or small as you'd like. Donate to charity, volunteer your time, or even just do the dishes without your parents asking. Shovel someone's driveway or visit someone you know who will be alone this holiday season." This request was on Becca's bucket list of things to do before she died of her illness.

The reaction to Becca's post was amazing. Beginning with friends and neighbours, responses to her request quickly spread across Canada, the United States, and as far away as Kuwait, Japan, and Australia. On Facebook and Twitter, people posted their random acts of kindness, from small to big, and tagged them with #BeccaToldMeTo.

Many of the posts mentioned simple acts of kindness: posters had bought a coffee or even paid for the whole order of the person behind them in line at fast food restaurants (especially Tim Hortons); purchased a turkey or presents for strangers at Christmas; bought a meal for a homeless person or delivered one to a housebound senior; gave warm clothes to homeless people or various charities that helped them; donated money or goods to animal shelters; and several hundred more gestures of compassion.

On her Facebook page, titled "Becca's Battle with Butterscotch," Becca wrote an inspiring message: "Please try to think less of how my life will be cut short and more of how wicked awesome my time left will be."

Becca's reach was international. In appreciation of her ability to mobilize people around the world to do good deeds, Becca was recognized with several honours. Among others, she received an RCMP Commander's Certificate of Appreciation for Outstanding Community Spirit and Leadership, had an annual Becca Schofield Day proclaimed by New Brunswick for the third Saturday every September, and received both the Canada 150 Senate Medal and a Meritorious Service Medal (Civil Division)—which entitled Becca to use the post-nominal "MSM"—from the Governor General on October 17, 2017.

The citation for Becca's MSM reads:

> Recent high school graduate Becca Schofield has motivated people to perform random acts of kindness and post about them on social media using the hashtag #BeccaToldMeTo. In a

blog about her battle with cancer, she wrote that encouraging more kindness in the world was at the top of her "bucket list." Her courage and generous nature are an inspiration to her peers, her community and millions of others around the globe.

Sadly, despite the best efforts of doctors, tremendous community support, and Becca's fighting spirit, she died of her illness on February 17, 2018.

On August 6, 2018, the New Brunswick government announced the posthumous award of the Order of New Brunswick to Becca for "inspiring New Brunswickers to be kind to each other and uniting the province through selfless acts of compassion and generosity." This award also allows the post-nominal "ONB" to be used after Becca's name, following the "MSM." These are two great honours indeed for a very courageous young lady.

Later in August 2018, the town of Riverview announced a playground, formerly known as All World Super Play Park, would be upgraded to include increased accessibility and a toddler play area. It was renamed the Rebecca Schofield All World Super Play Park, and was officially opened in June 2019. To help with fundraising, Dairy Queen New Brunswick launched a "Buy a Cake for Becca" campaign on September 1—Becca's birthday. For twenty-five dollars, customers could buy a voucher for an ice cream cake, with proceeds going towards the park. Additionally, prior to Becca Schofield Day 2018, all students in the province received a kindness card. The card asked them to perform an act of kindness in Becca's name and pass the card on, in the hopes the recipient would also carry out an act of kindness and pass the card on to someone else.

We can only hope the outstanding initiative Becca started continues to spread.

# CHAPTER 9

# SEAFARERS

Most Atlantic Canadians are never far from salt water. All four provinces have lengthy coastlines, either directly on the ocean or along gulfs, bays, and other inlets. Although Atlantic Canada represents only 5.4 percent of the country's land mass, it includes 13.6 percent of the national coastline, which is the longest in the world!

The sea defines much of the Atlantic provinces, from the natural history elements of geology, geography, climate, flora, and fauna, to the human history components of people, settlement, economy, and industry. Many say the sea is in the blood of Atlantic Canadians. It is not surprising, then, that many Atlantic stories—both fact and fiction—are connected to the sea in some way.

# FATHER OF THE ROYAL NAVY

Provo William Parry Wallis was born in Halifax, Nova Scotia, on April, 12, 1791, the only son of the clerk of the dockyard's master shipwright in the town's important Royal Navy Dockyard. Provo's father wanted a naval career for his son and knew the rules around officers joining the Royal Navy at an early age.

On May 1, 1795, his father managed to get Provo officially registered as an able-bodied seaman when he was only four years old. He was officially on the books of the thirty-six-gun frigate *Oiseau*. This purpose of this paper transaction was to get around the regulation that all potential lieutenants (the lowest officer rank) had to have served at least six years at sea, including two as a midshipman (an apprentice officer). Recording young boys as seamen or captain's servants to gain the required experience—at least on paper—was a common practice.

Young Provo moved through other ships (still on paper) during the next few years. Thanks to his father, by the time Provo finished his schooling in England and actually reported on board his first real ship, he had nearly a decade of seniority behind him. He joined the *Cleopatra* at Portsmouth, England, in October 1804 as a thirteen-year-old midshipman. At the time, England and France were at war.

Under the command of Captain Sir Robert Lowrie, *Cleopatra* sailed for the West Indies and spent some time there. On February 17, 1805, Captain Lowrie was returning to England when the forty-gun French frigate *Ville de Milan* was spotted off Bermuda. The French ship was on its way from the island of Martinique to France. Although Lowrie realized the French ship was superior to his, he ordered a chase. At the same time, the French captain was under orders not to engage other ships, so he raised extra sails to increase his speed and escape. The chase continued for almost three hundred kilometres and lasted into the next morning.

As *Cleopatra* gained on *Ville de Milan*, the French ship came about to face its English enemy. The battle began at about two-thirty in the afternoon. For the next two and a half hours a heavy cannonade was kept up between the two ships.

Then, around five o'clock, Captain Lowrie attempted to cross the enemy vessel's bow to rake it with cannon fire, but a French cannon ball destroyed *Cleopatra*'s wheel and then its rudder jammed. Once *Cleopatra* became unmanoeuverable, *Ville de Milan* closed to board, and rammed *Cleopatra* while French musket fire raked the English ship's deck. Although *Cleopatra*'s sailors successfully fought off the first French attempt to board, they could not break their ship free.

A second boarding attempt by the French succeeded. By now, *Cleopatra* had lost several masts and a third of her crew. Lowrie hauled down his flag—the naval way to indicate surrender. Both ships were heavily damaged and the French captain was killed, along with several of his crewmen. At thirteen years of age, Provo Wallis was now a prisoner of war.

The French spent the next three days transferring some of their new English prisoners to the French ship, and putting some French sailors on the English ship to sail it to France. At the same time, they completed essential repairs to both ships. On February 21, the two ships got under weigh.

Two days later, the ships were spotted by the Royal Navy's fifty-two-gun *Leander* under Captain John Talbot. *Leander* pressed down on them, causing them to separate. Talbot chased *Cleopatra*, forced it to stop, and recaptured the English ship. Provo was freed.

*Leander* then pursued *Ville de Milan* and overtook it. The French ship surrendered without a fight. Captain Talbot took both ships to Halifax, Nova Scotia, where *Ville de Milan* was taken into the Royal Navy as a British ship—HMS *Milan*. Provo was initially transferred to *Milan* and a little over a year later, in November 1806, he moved to *Triumph* as acting lieutenant. He was not yet sixteen.

Provo went on to an illustrious naval career. He was promoted to lieutenant at seventeen and ended up serving in the frigate *Shannon* in January 1812. *Shannon* captured the American frigate USS *Chesapeake* in June 1813 after a ferocious battle off Boston, Massachusetts, during the War of 1812. It was one of the bloodiest ship-on-ship actions in history.

Because *Shannon*'s captain was severely wounded and the first lieutenant was killed in the action, Provo served as acting captain of the ship for exactly six days. Under Provo, *Shannon* made its way back to Halifax, with the captured *Chesapeake* behind, flying the English Blue Ensign above the Stars and Stripes.

Provo rose steadily through the officer ranks to the highest rank of admiral. In order to prevent admirals from dying in poverty, a special clause in a new retirement scheme in 1870 provided that those officers who had commanded a ship before the end of the Napoleonic Wars (of which the War of 1812 was the North American part) should be retained on the active list. The six days Provo was in command of HMS *Shannon* qualified him to remain on the active list until he died. Remaining on the active list meant he could to be called up for a seagoing command at any point. Even when naval headquarters suggested he retire in his late nineties and avoid the active list, Provo replied he was ready to accept any mission.

He was promoted to Admiral of the Fleet in December 1875, the highest position in the Royal Navy. When he died on February 13, 1892, just two months before his 101st birthday, Provo had served an incredible ninety-six years in the Royal Navy and was known as "The Father of the British Fleet."

Between 1969 and 2006, the Canadian Coast Guard Ship *Provo Wallis* operated on the Atlantic coast, with its home port at Saint John, New Brunswick. It was then transferred to the west coast for it final years of service until it was decommissioned in 2010.

# THE ONLY CHILD TO SURVIVE

In the spring of 1873, the Royal Mail Ship (RMS) *Atlantic* was on her nineteenth voyage from Liverpool, England, to New York, with more than nine hundred people on board. *Atlantic* was a modern, state-of-the-art ship for its time. It was metal-hulled and powered by steam with sails for backup, and with a propeller instead of the paddle wheels most steamships of the day used.

After steaming past Halifax, Nova Scotia, Captain James Williams decided to turn around and put in to Halifax Harbour. He thought coal might be running short after they had encountered a lengthy storm during the crossing, and was afraid there might not be enough to reach New York. After he gave the order to turn back toward Halifax, Williams went to bed. With the captain asleep, the officers he left in charge made a series of navigation errors that put them twenty kilometres off course.

As a result, *Atlantic* struck a granite ledge off the tiny fishing village of Lower Prospect, Nova Scotia, a few kilometres southwest of Halifax, at 3:15 A.M. on April 1. The crew lowered all ten lifeboats, but they were immediately washed away or smashed to pieces. Within minutes, *Atlantic*'s stern sank and the ship heeled to port and filled with water, drowning hundreds of passengers and crew in their beds almost instantly.

Some people tried to swim ashore, but the huge waves and freezing water were too much. Although most who tried to swim ashore drowned, a few hardy sailors managed to make it, towing ropes called lifelines from the ship. The seamen tied these lifelines around big rocks, and some of those still aboard *Atlantic* climbed the rigging into the masts with the other ends of the lines. But it was the middle of the night in early spring, and they were exposed and poorly dressed.

Once their hands became numb and their strength ebbed with the cold, most lost their grip and fell into the surging waves below. Some of the stronger men managed to crawl hand-over-hand along the lifelines. Few made it.

The residents of Lower Prospect had heard the commotion and soon arrived to offer shelter to anyone who managed to struggle ashore. At daybreak, some local men braved high waves and put their small boats in the water in an attempt to rescue more survivors.

All the women, all the married men, and all the children—except for one—perished. It's hard to know exactly how many died, but estimates range from 535 to almost 600. The only child to survive was twelve-year-old John Hindley. He was emigrating from England with his parents and older brother to join his two married sisters in New Jersey.

John had been awakened by the great noise of the ship hitting rocks and got up to see what was happening. When the ship suddenly tipped over, he followed some men and managed to stay above the rapidly rising water. The men broke open a porthole and someone pushed the boy out and yelled at him to climb up and hang onto the rigging. He did so and bravely managed to hang on for the rest of the night, until he was rescued the next morning by local fishermen.

Although John survived, his mother, father, and brother died. The terrible tragedy and loss of life he witnessed was a heavy burden for a twelve-year-old boy—the only child to survive—to bear. That could be the reason that John had a hard life and passed away at age twenty-nine.

⟜◦◦◦⟜

The wreck of the SS *Atlantic* was the deadliest civilian maritime disaster in the North Atlantic Ocean until the *Titanic* sank in 1912. Today, you can visit the SS *Atlantic* Heritage Interpretation Park in Terrence Bay, Nova Scotia. The seaside park is maintained by volunteers who restore the burial sites and monuments, while preserving the history of this tragedy.

# SAVING DOLPHINS

In February 2009, the residents of Seal Cove, Newfoundland and Labrador—a town of some three hundred people northwest of St. John's—had been going to bed each night with the wails of five white-beaked dolphins echoing in their ears. The dolphins had been trapped in the ice in the cove for several days, swimming in smaller and smaller circles as the ice closed in on them.

As the dolphins continued to cry for help, some townspeople went down to the cove at night with spotlights. They even tried to get a government icebreaker to break a path through the ice, but no ships were available. Even if one had been available, it might have accidentally pushed ice into the struggling animals, injuring or killing them.

Then a few local fishermen decided to act. Sixteen-year-old Brandon Banks and four others dug a fibreglass boat out from the snow. Brandon and a couple of the others put on bright red survival suits and began chopping through the ice to make a 250-metre-long path for the dolphins to open water.

It took about three hours to clear a path through the ice and two of the five dolphins—two had died—swam to the ocean. The last one was too exhausted to swim and most people believed it would not survive the night. Something had to be done—and fast.

Brandon jumped into the frigid ocean water. He held the head of the 176-pound dolphin above the water, got a rope around the animal, and tied the rope to the boat. The dolphin seemed to sense what Brandon was trying to do and wrapped its flippers around the teenager while he got everything in place. The boat then towed the dolphin slowly to open water, where it got its second wind and swam free.

In saving the dolphins, Brandon and the residents of Seal Cove performed a particularly appropriate act. For thousands of years, dolphins have been known to come to the rescue of humans in distress in the water. In particular, dolphins have helped drowning sailors and have protected people from shark attacks.

# AROUND THE ISLAND

It took eleven days of paddling for a sixteen-year-old from Bonshaw, Prince Edward Island, to kayak the perimeter of his province in August 2016, covering about 550 kilometres. Travelling alone, Joe Simmonds camped along the way, usually on beaches.

It was the first time Joe had ever done an overnight trip since first buying a kayak when he was twelve, using money he had earned selling worms as bait. Before his round-the-island trip he had only made day trips and wanted a more adventurous challenge—yet one that was still manageable.

To prepare for the voyage, Joe trained with regular two-to-four-hour trips in the nearby Bonshaw River. To earn money for the equipment he would need, Joe did odd jobs for his parents, such as painting. He purchased a good life jacket, an extra paddle, and a waterproof telephone that could float. He also bought a journal, as well as a waterproof Bible.

Although Joe's mother, Jessica, supported her son from the start, his father, Jonathan, was not so sure Joe was up to the challenge. Eventually, Joe won his father over. He convinced him he had the commitment, responsibility, and ability to organize, undertake, and complete the journey.

Due to wind and weather considerations, Joe paddled counter-clockwise around the island. Despite this precaution, he still missed one day due to dangerous seas, which turned it into a twelve-day trip. He had GPS to confirm his location and checked in by cellphone each morning before he began the day's ten-to-twelve-hour paddle and each evening after he hauled his kayak onto a beach and set up his camp.

Breakfast each day was what Joe described to a reporter later as a "really, really gross protein shake," while lunch consisted of dried fruit and meat, and chocolate bars (he ate more than fifty Snickers bars during the trip). Supper was instant meals, prepared by adding boiling water to such dried foods as rice, macaroni and cheese, and powdered soups. Halfway through his trip, Joe's parents met him at Cavendish Beach with fresh supplies. The daily exercise and limited diet resulted in Joe losing more than eight pounds. He ate "constantly" at home in the days following his trip.

About halfway through the trip, one of the foot braces in Joe's kayak broke. Two days later, his kayak capsized, tossing Joe into the sea and leaving him unable to climb back in. He had to swim ashore with the kayak and regroup. Luckily, he did not lose any critical supplies.

With only brief telephone conversations with his parents, Joe had a lot of time to think. He sang hymns and felt a very spiritual, peaceful connection with his surroundings. "I really felt close to God," he told CBC News reporter Natalia Goodwin shortly after his journey, adding, "When the big waves come you realize how helpless you are and how dependent you are on God, so I really got a sense of that."

In addition to the physical hardship—especially the blisters on his hands and feet—Joe also had to cope with hunger and homesickness. He found it very lonely being by himself for twelve days. If he ever does it again, he says he'll bring a companion along for company. A year after his voyage in 2017, Joe wrote a book about his adventure, called *Boy Afloat: Kayaking Solo Around Prince Edward Island.*

# CHAPTER 10

# SUPER GIRLS

For centuries—with rare exceptions—only men were celebrated as achievers. It was widely believed that a woman's place was in the home, keeping house and raising children. Equality between men and women is a relatively modern concept. For example, Canadian women have only been allowed to vote in federal elections since 1918. Provincially, it occurred in Nova Scotia the same year, in New Brunswick in 1919, in Prince Edward Island in 1922, and in Newfoundland it was not until 1925.

Since then, women's achievements have expanded year after year. Whether it is athletics, science, or adventuring, girls are doing amazing things around the world and here at home. There are still plenty of struggles women and girls face—and particularly women of colour and trans women—but as you will see in these next pages, it does not stop them from achieving amazing things.

# THE RUNNER

A descendant of United Empire Loyalists—people who remained loyal to the British Crown during the American Revolutionary War and came to Canada—Marjorie Turner-Bailey grew up in the small Nova Scotia fishing village of Lockeport. There, she was one of four children in the community's only black family.

Marjorie was a great athlete. She loved sports and played with her sisters on the Lockeport Regional High School basketball team. In 1964, when she was sixteen, her team won the provincial championship. She was also a star player on the school's soccer team. In a brief account of her life published in 2017, Marjorie wrote that coming "from a very small fishing town" she was "fortunate to be able to excel in sports" as "there was nothing else to do in Lockeport." And excel in sports she did—setting records in the process

That same year, Eldon Forbes, a new physical education teacher at Marjorie's high school, wanted to know if any students would like to take part in track and field, a new sport for the school. Although Marjorie admitted she did not know much about track and field, once she learned about the various events, she and half a dozen other students decided to try it. At the same time, Marjorie happened to read an article about an American relay team and their success, which influenced her decision to try out. Since there were no tracks in Lockeport at the time, Marjorie ran sprints on the local beach at low tide—impressive resistance training!

From having no experience with track and field events, Marjorie became one of the youngest Canadians ever to qualify for the Olympics—while she was still a high school student.

Her meteoric rise began with the Mount Allison University Invitational in Sackville, New Brunswick, in the spring of 1964 when she was in grade eleven. Lockeport High had never participated in this event before, but Eldon Forbes and principal Louis Fraser petitioned the school board to let them enter a team. Fortunately, for the school and Marjorie, the board members agreed—and history was made.

At Mount Allison, Marjorie led Lockeport High to the championship title when she won *all* the running and field events she entered. Later that spring, on June 1, as her school's only representative at the Acadia Relays at Acadia University in Wolfville, Nova Scotia—the biggest track and field event in the province—Marjorie continued winning. She came first in the girls' "A" 100- and 220-yard dashes, javelin, and discus. Her time of 11.6 seconds for the 100 yards tied the record for the meet. Additionally, her single-day total of twenty-eight points was the highest for the day and won the class "A" provincial title for her school. The speed, strength, and endurance of this newcomer surprised everyone. Malcolm Johnson, writing in the *Halifax Chronicle-Herald* about Marjorie's June 1 performance, described her as a "one-girl track and field team," while Kentville sport historian Burton Russell called her "mercury-footed."

At Greenwood, Nova Scotia, Marjorie equalled the provincial record for the 100-yard dash with a time of 11.2 seconds—a record established in 1935 by an Olympic sprinter. At Summerside, Prince Edward Island, at the Eastern Canadian Championships, Marjorie set a new Canadian record for the 100-yard dash with a time of 10.8 seconds. Although she had strained a thigh muscle during that event, Marjorie went on to win the 220-yard race.

Later that summer, at the Canadian Olympic Time Trials in St. Lambert, Quebec, she ran the 100 yards in 12 seconds. Her second-place finish secured her a coveted spot on the national team for the 1964 Tokyo Summer Olympics.

Marjorie was named Nova Scotia's Athlete of the Year in 1964—and she was only sixteen. She also received the Myrtle Cook Trophy for Young Athlete of the Year, named after famed Canadian athlete and women's sports journalist Myrtle Cook. Additionally, she has the unique distinction of being inducted into both the Nova Scotia and British Columbia Sports Halls of Fame.

Although Marjorie had qualified for the 1964 Tokyo Olympics, leg and back injuries prevented her from participating. She was able to compete in the 1966 Commonwealth Games in Kingston, Jamaica; however, injury also stopped her from attending the Mexico City Olympics in 1968. Later she was able to participate in other events on the international stage. She won two bronze medals at the 1975 Pan Am Games, and represented Canada at the 1976 Montreal Olympics, where she helped her relay team set a Canadian record.

Marjorie retired from athletics in 1978, after winning a silver medal at the Edmonton Commonwealth Games.

# MARJORIE'S INTERNATIONAL ATHLETIC ACHIEVEMENTS

*Note:* International sports competitions once used imperial measurements, such as yards, but now use metric measurements, such as metres.

## OLYMPIC GAMES

- 1976 Montreal: fourth in 4 x 100-metre relay (which set Canadian record of 43.17 seconds); reached semifinal in 100 metres, semifinal in 200 metres.

## COMMONWEALTH GAMES

- 1966 Kingston, Jamaica: fourth in 4 × 440-yard relay
- 1974 Christchurch, New Zealand: fourth in 200 metres, fourth in 4 × 100-metre relay, sixth in 100 metres.
- 1978 Edmonton, Alberta: silver medal in 4 × 100-metre relay, fourth in 200 metres.

## PAN AMERICAN GAMES

- 1975 Mexico City, Mexico: bronze medal in 100 metres, bronze medal in 4 × 100-metre relay, fourth in 200 metres.

# THE INVENTOR

One day in 2013, eleven-year-old Rachel Brouwer, then a grade eight student at Bedford Academy, had an idea with the potential to directly affect the lives of millions of people. At the time, she was on a holiday with her family in New Hampshire and she and her brother, Mitchell, were out hiking.

As they walked through the hills and past rivers and lakes, they noticed several signs that read "Contaminated: Do Not Drink." Rachel had always loved making crafts and was interested in figuring out how things worked. Now she put her mind to work on the problem of contaminated water.

At the same time, Rachel was reading *I Am Malala* by Pakistani activist Malala Yousafzai. In 2012, when she was just fifteen years old, Malala had been shot in the head by Taliban terrorists for promoting girls' education. In Malala's book, she wrote about many people dying from a waterborne disease called cholera. Rachel was inspired and began to research ideas to purify drinking water.

That is when Rachel conceived of a water filter. But after several months of trial and error, she realized a filter would not be enough. Although it removed impurities such as dirt, sand, and clay, it did nothing about the bacteria present in the water.

Bacteria in water causes many diseases, so Rachel studied methods of killing bacteria. That was when she learned about solar pasteurization, which uses the power of the sun to heat water to 60 degrees Celsius—the temperature at which bacteria dies. Rachel thought if she could use things like pipes, two-litre water bottles, cotton, and charcoal, her system would be useful in developing countries where those items are common. She even designed a simple hand pump to make it easier to draw water into the bottles.

Rachel found that putting the bottles on the corrugated tin roofs that are found in many hot countries helped the water to reach the necessary temperature. Generally, six hours in direct sunlight or two days of cloudy weather are enough to reach the proper temperature for her filter to work.

In some countries, however, the sun cannot heat water to the 60 degrees necessary to kill bacteria. That was when Rachel discovered that the sun's ultraviolet radiation can also be used to inactivate bacteria in water if heat alone does not do the trick.

To know when the water temperature reaches 60 degrees, she also designed an indicator that shows when the water is safe to drink. The indicator is made of soybean wax and changes colour, from dark blue to light pink, as the water changes temperature. When the wax melts—at 60 degrees—and drips to a second chamber, the water is ready.

Rachel tested her system using E. coli—a common bacteria that is the cause of water contamination in many parts of the world. She found her system eliminated all of the E. coli in her contaminated samples.

Rachel first exhibited her system at the Halifax Science Expo in 2014. In May 2016, when she was fourteen and in grade nine, her invention won a gold medal at the annual Canada-Wide Science Fair and also won the Best Junior Environmental Project Challenge. That same month, Rachel was one of just eight Canadian students to enter projects in the Intel International Science and Engineering Fair, held in Phoenix, Arizona. Almost two thousand young scientists from seventy-seven countries competed in the event. Rachel came second in the Earth and Environmental Sciences category. Her prize was $1,500 and having an asteroid named after her: the Rachel Brouwer of Bedford Academy.

Rachel also received an inspirational email from her role model, Malala, before the competition. "Thank you for your great work and ambition and determination," it read. "Nothing can stop you. Believe in yourself and keep on moving." Two years earlier, Malala had been awarded the Nobel Peace Prize for her own work as an advocate for the rights of women and children.

In 2015, Rachel began to be recognized for her work by winning many different awards. She was awarded the Youth Discovery Award, Community Hero Award, the Bedford Youth Volunteer Award, and the Nova Scotia Red Cross Youth Humanitarian Award. The next year, she received the Youth Women's Excellence and Youth Provincial Volunteer Awards.

Rachel's invention is already being used in Uganda, where schoolkids sent her a video thanking her for sharing her system, saying they "are no longer thirsty." She hopes to have the system tested in other countries soon.

Rachel has been raising money to have her water-purification system patented, which legally stops anyone from copying her filter without her permission. During an interview in June 2015 with Katy Parsons of CBC News, she said, "It's really exciting to know the system is actually making a difference. It's really, like, a dream come true."

Rachel's latest project is the development of an open-source 3D printer platform, where kids within the Halifax Regional Centre for Education can share their 3D designs with teachers, educators, and students. This will provide kids who have ideas similar to Rachel's a place to connect and work together. Rachel will include the design for her wax indicator on the platform, so anyone can print it in 3D and learn about the water purification process. With the platform, there will be a chapter of Enabling the Future, an international group of 3D printer enthusiasts who create free 3D-printed hand and arm prosthetics for those who need them. Rachel's teacher, Jonah Scott, is assisting her with the logistics of this project, for which Rachel is very grateful. "He is a huge help!" she notes.

But it's not all work. Like other kids her age, Rachel enjoys many hobbies and activities, such as basketball and soccer. She also developed her own line of skincare products, the profits of which she donated to Halifax's IWK children's hospital.

For the future, Rachel plans to attend university to study environmental sciences. She has not decided on a university yet, but if her program would allow her to travel to Africa for environmental research, Rachel says that would be a big factor in her decision.

# THE SCIENTIST

It came as a shock to eleven-year-old Stella Bowles in 2015 when she discovered the beautiful river that flowed by her house was too polluted to swim in. The LaHave River runs from Nova Scotia's Annapolis Valley to the South Shore. During its ninety-seven-kilometre journey to the ocean, the river winds through several communities, including Stella's village of Upper LaHave.

The technical term for the type of pollution in the LaHave River is "fecal contamination," which is caused by the bacteria in human waste, known as feces. Stella had a more direct name for it: poop. That's right—the pollution was caused by residents along the river flushing their toilets directly into it through so-called straight pipes, without any treatment. In fact, about six hundred houses sent the contents of their toilets into the river every day. No wonder the river was polluted!

Stella was disgusted. When her mom, Andrea, was growing up, the Nova Scotia Department of Health tested the river water regularly and put up signs reading *No Swimming. Fecal Contamination.* Then one day the signs disappeared. Despite the contamination, many people continued to wade and swim in the river or sail on it, occasionally falling in. Stella had not heard any stories of anyone getting sick from this, so her first task was to find out if there was enough poop in the water to make someone ill.

Stella found out about David Maxwell, a retired doctor who lived on the LaHave River and had been testing the river for fecal contamination for more than two years. Although Dr. Maxwell had reported the results of his tests to various levels of government, no one had done anything about it. Even the LaHave River Straight Pipe Committee to which he belonged was unable to prod the government into action.

Then Stella had an idea. If the government would not put up a sign warning about the contamination, she would. With her dad's help, Stella designed and built a big sign, which they put on their property beside the road and the river. In big, bold letters, it read:

People noticed the sign immediately and it soon became a hot topic in the area. But Stella wanted to spread the word to more people, not just those who noticed the sign. Reluctantly—concerned about possible negative comments—her mother started a Facebook group about Stella's project.

After she started grade six, Stella attended a meeting of the Straight Pipe Committee. Its members were frustrated. They had been bringing the issue to the Nova Scotia government for more than two years, only to receive promises that were later broken. Stella wondered if a kid could do any better. She decided to study the river contamination for her grade six science project that March.

Stella knew she first had to test the river water, which would be an expensive task. It cost thirty dollars for each test, and several tests at different locations along the river would be required. Her mom contacted Dr. Maxwell for advice and he agreed to talk to Stella in October.

At the meeting, Dr. Maxwell explained what Stella would be testing for: a bacteria called enterococci. It lives in the intestines of warm-blooded animals, and ends up in their waste. Dr. Maxwell gave Stella two important numbers: 70 or more enterococci per 100 millilitres of water meant it was unsafe for swimming in Canada (although many American beaches use a lower level of 35).

If there were 175 or more, it meant the water should not come into contact with skin. Such contact could cause a number of conditions, among them a rash, an itch, or an ear infection. Stella memorized these numbers. In the LaHave River, the levels were almost always above 70 and usually above 175.

The best way to prevent further fecal contamination was to replace all the straight pipes with septic systems. Such systems are common throughout rural Canada. Basically, through a network of underground pipes and a tank, these systems allow organisms in the ground to destroy the harmful bacteria before it reaches the river. And even though straight pipes are now illegal, replacing them with expensive septic systems was not enforced by the government.

Dr. Maxwell told Stella she could reduce the cost of water testing by doing it herself. Fortunately, he had extra equipment, as well as an incubator that would allow her to grow fecal colonies from the water samples. When Dr. Maxwell delivered the equipment to Stella in November, he explained the procedures to draw and test the water, showed her how to use the equipment properly, and how to sterilize her tap water, which would be the control sample against which she would compare the river water. It was a lot of information for Stella to absorb, but Dr. Maxwell promised to be there each step of the way. He suggested she choose four sites along the river to draw her samples from, and decide if she would do it at high or low tide. Whatever she selected, she had to be consistent each time she gathered samples.

Stella's first test results from the four sites were shocking, ranging from a low of 147 enterococci per 100 millilitres to a high of 3,020. When this was posted on her Facebook page, the results went viral and CBC conducted a radio interview.

Further results confirmed Stella's initial findings. When some people commented the contamination could come from duck poop instead of human, Stella remembered all the gross things she had seen in the river, especially where the straight pipes emptied into the water. Her reply was simple: "The last time I looked, ducks don't use toilet paper."

Stella's school project on contamination in the LaHave River was one of ten chosen to go to the regional science fair. A CBC TV interview followed. When it aired, it also included an interview with the mayor of the Municipality of Lunenburg, who supported Stella's call to clean up the river.

To get money to replace the straight pipes with septic systems required that each level of government—municipal, provincial, and federal—share the cost, which was estimated at more than $13 million. The municipality's third of the funding would be a loan that homeowners had to repay. At various public information sessions around the municipality, people generally agreed with the idea of eliminating straight pipes, but could not agree on how to do it fairly. Meanwhile, Stella's entry at the regional science fair won a gold medal.

At a municipal council meeting in June 2016—filmed by both CBC and CTV—all but one councillor voted to replace the straight pipes. Three weeks later, the Municipality of Lunenburg and the Province of Nova Scotia signed an agreement to eliminate straight pipes along the LaHave River. Although the federal government had not yet signed on, the local Member of Parliament promised her support.

While Stella and her family waited for news of federal government funding, she made it to the regional science fair with an updated and expanded grade seven project about the contamination. This also won her a place on the provincial team representing Nova Scotia at the Canada-Wide Science Fair in Regina, Saskatchewan, at which she won a silver medal.

But Stella was disappointed the federal government had still not committed to the project. It had been twenty-one months since she had started testing and during that time an additional 600,000 litres of waste water had been flushed into the LaHave every day. Stella decided to make a new sign to get people's attention, this time with even bigger letters. It read:

> # 600+ HOMES FLUSH THEIR TOILETS DIRECTLY INTO THIS RIVER

Then, on June 29, 2017, the exciting news arrived: the federal government announced it would provide its one-third portion. The LaHave River would be straight-pipe free in six years! Once funding was assured, Stella took her sign down.

Stella's work has been acknowledged with several awards. She was named one of Canada's Top 25 Environmentalists Under 25 and received both the Evergreen Toronto Dominion Bank Future City Builder Award and the Wade Luzny Youth Conservation Award from the Canadian Wildlife Federation. She also placed first in her age group (thirteen to sixteen) as a 2018 International Young Eco-Hero.

In 2018, Stella was awarded a Meritorious Service Medal (Civil Division) by the Governor General. Her citation reads:

> Elementary school student Stella Bowles studied the contamination of the LaHave River near her home for a science project. When she discovered that untreated sewage was polluting the river, she used social media to gather support to have it cleaned up. As her online following grew, the media took notice and, eventually, all three levels of government pledged funds toward improving the water quality.

Stella wrote a book about her successful campaign to replace all straight pipes along the LaHave River, titled *My River: Cleaning up the LaHave River*, proving even a kid can initiate a major change.

# THE ADVENTURER

When Olivia Gourley of Stewiacke, Nova Scotia, was only twelve years old, she and her father went on a five-day South American adventure that took her to the fabled Peruvian city of Machu Picchu. Olivia and her father hiked high into the Andes Mountains, where the rarified air often causes altitude sickness. Rather than use the conventional (and easier) tourist route, their difficult trek took them through the Salkantay Pass on the Inca Trail.

This hike would have been impressive for any twelve year old, but it was especially impressive because Olivia had undergone spinal surgery just a year earlier. She had begun experiencing back pain when she was eleven, but thought it was due to being involved in several sports. One day her back became so sore she had to be carried off the soccer field.

Shortly afterwards she went to a chiropractor, who diagnosed her condition as soon as she lay down on the table. "You've got scoliosis," he said. Olivia was terrified: what the heck is scoliosis? She soon found out: it is a condition that causes a sideways curve of the spine, it most often occurs during the growth spurt just before puberty, and it affects girls more severely than boys. If left untreated, the curvature would become worse.

So Olivia underwent groundbreaking surgery at Halifax's famed IWK Health Centre. The operation involved putting eight screws into the right side of her backbone and attaching a flexible cord to them. Over time, the cord will straighten her backbone as it grows. The operation took ten hours and involved deflating her right lung, which added to her recovery time.

Fortunately, Olivia was very fit and eight months after surgery she was playing soccer and hockey again. Two years later, besides soccer and hockey, she added badminton, volleyball, track and field, and CrossFit workouts. She also runs five days a week. On top of her sports, Olivia maintains an excellent academic record. She was Student of the Year in 2013 and she has received leadership awards and honours for her 95 percent average.

After Machu Picchu, next on Olivia's adventure list is one of the most forbidding places on earth: Antarctica. Not only are she and her dad, Chris—an experienced mountain climber—going to travel to the snow- and ice-bound continent, they plan to ski to the South Pole.

After a twenty-hour journey from Halifax to Chile, at the southern tip of South America, a four-and-half-hour flight onboard a transport plane will carry them to an ice runway on Antarctica's Union Glacier. The overland trek will involve a tough two-to-three-week journey on skis, travelling for about ten hours a day.

Such a journey has been made by very few people—and none as young as Olivia. The slog halfway across the uninhabited landscape will involve overcoming brutally cold temperatures that can reach minus 40 degrees Celcius, treacherous snow conditions, and altitudes higher than 2,800 metres—not to mention the mental challenge of isolation and the physical hardship.

The training schedule that Olivia's dad set up to prepare is punishing. One of the exercises consists of hauling a heavy tire and rim along dirt roads with a harness. This simulates pulling a sledge with 99 pounds of essential gear on it—only slightly less than the fourteen year old's weight of 110 pounds. The father-daughter duo will have to haul everything they need for their journey, including a tent, sleeping bags, spare skis, food, fuel, and communication devices. In order to finance the trip, Olivia and her dad have set a fundraising goal of $100,000, which they hope will come from both individual donors and corporate sponsorships.

Olivia likes to challenge herself, but as she stated in an online video for the *Truro News* in August 2018, she also wants "to show young women they shouldn't limit themselves to what they can achieve. That they can set high goals for themselves and they can achieve those goals if they're willing to put in the work and be dedicated to it." She also feels people "don't have to fall into society's expectations of what they can do, because that's really up to them."

# FURTHER READING

The stories of the amazing kids in this book were based on a variety of sources, including books, newspaper and magazine articles, websites, and interviews. If you're interested in learning more about some of the amazing kids profiled in this book, listed below are the books—some for children and some for adults—used in researching these stories.

Bailey-Turner, Marjorie. *Marjorie Turner-Bailey Can Run: Her Journal.* Yarmouth, NS: Seeblick Printing, 2017.

Black, Dan, and John Boileau. *Old Enough to Fight: Canada's Boy Soldiers in the First World War.* Toronto: Lorimer Publishing, 2013.

Boileau, John. *Valiant Hearts: Atlantic Canada and the Victoria Cross.* Halifax: Nimbus Publishing, 2005.

Boileau, John. *6•12•17: The Halifax Explosion.* Lunenburg, NS: MacIntyre Purcell Publishing, 2017.

Bowes, Stella, with Anne Laurel Carter. *My River: Cleaning up the LaHave River.* Halifax: Formac Publishing, 2018.

Brown, Roger David. *Blood on the Coal: The Story of the Springhill Mining Disasters.* Halifax: Nimbus Publishing, 2002.

Cochkanoff, Greg, and Bob Chaulk. *SS Atlantic: The White Star Line's First Disaster at Sea*. Fredericton, NB: Goose Lane, 2009.

DeGarthe, William E. *This is Peggy's Cove*. Self-published: 1984.

Dickie, John R. *Age of Heroes: A Boy, a Prince and the 1797 Wreck of La Tribune*. Lawrencetown, NS: Pottersfield Press, 2009.

Montgomery, L. M. *Anne of Green Gables*. Boston, MA: L. C. Page & Co., 1908.

Ruck, Calvin W. *The Black Battalion 1916–1920: Canada's Best Kept Military Secret*. Halifax: Nimbus Publishing, 1986.

Simmonds, Joseph Ian. *Boy Afloat: Kayaking Solo Around Prince Edward Island*. Scotts Valley, CA: CreateSpace, 2017.

Tremere, Jason, ed., *#BeccaToldMeTo: Spreading kindness, one hashtag at a time*. Scotts Valley, CA: CreateSpace, 2017.

Wade, Mamadou and the youth of Hope Blooms. *Hope Blooms: Plant a Seed, Harvest a Dream*. Halifax: Nimbus Publishing, 2018.

Walsh, Alice. *Heroes of Isle aux Morts*. Toronto: Tundra Books, 2001.

# ACKNOWLEDGEMENTS

No work of non-fiction is ever written in isolation. Writers depend upon a vast array of reference materials, largely consisting of the printed word—books, magazines, newspapers, journals, and diaries—but also on personal interviews. I have used all of these sources in writing this book and I am most grateful to those who provided them.

The idea for such a book came from Nova Scotia artist and illustrator Richard Rudnicki. In mid-March 2015, Richard and I first met during a meeting of the No. 2 Construction Battalion Centennial Planning Committee in the Black Cultural Centre in Cherry Brook, Nova Scotia, while I was there in a historical advisory capacity.

Richard approached me and asked if I would like to write a children's book that he would illustrate. "Sure," I replied. "What's it about?" Richard then went on to explain his idea: a book detailing the lives of young Nova Scotians who had accomplished something extraordinary by the time they were fifteen or so.

I was immediately struck by this unique idea and devoted the next few weeks to researching suitable candidates. We approached Nimbus Publishing and received a favourable response, although Managing Editor Whitney Moran suggested a change: expand the stories to include not just Nova Scotia, but the other Atlantic provinces as well. After going back to the drawing board for more research, the expanded proposal was accepted by Nimbus and research began in earnest.

As with all my previous books published by Nimbus, it has once again been a pleasure working with Heather Bryan and Terrilee Bulger and, for the first time, with Whitney. I must also thank my editor, Emily MacKinnon, cover designer Jenn Embree, interior designer Peggy Issenman, and publicist Kate Watson at Nimbus for their valuable assistance in getting this book into print.

Unfortunately, Richard Rudnicki, who had proposed the idea in the first place, had to withdraw from illustrating the book due to other commitments and a move from Halifax to rural Nova Scotia. I owe a great debt of gratitude to Richard for conceiving this idea in the first place, asking me to write the text to accompany his illustrations, and then allowing me to carry on with his concept. In recognition of Richard's idea, the illustration that accompanies the story of Thomas Goffigan and the Black Battalion in Chapter Two is the one he created for the Army Museum–Halifax Citadel to commemorate the centennial of the unit. Many thanks to the museum's former vice-chair, Bruce Gilchrist, for granting me permission to use it.

Richard's replacement, James Bentley, was an excellent choice and he rose to the occasion. Working from the stories and sample images, James produced the outstanding illustrations, found throughout the book, that add so much to it.

On an individual level, I must also acknowledge the assistance of the following people, who graciously provided information about some of the kids profiled in this book: Jayson Baxter, Christopher and Olivia Gourley (Olivia Gourley); Linda Belliveau (Gage Gabriel); Brian Cuthbertson (Robert Kent); Pam

Publicover-Brouwer and Rachel Brouwer (Rachel Brouwer); Tammy and Olivia Mason (Olivia Mason); Maggie Peyton and Mohammad Al Maksour (Mohammad, Chaymaa, and Baraaa Marouf); Anne Schofield and Jason Tremere (Becca Schofield). Additional thanks goes to James Roberts of the National Film Board of Canada (since retired) for permission to tell the story of Maq, based on the NFB's 2006 animated short film *Maq and the Spirit of the Woods*, written and directed by Phyllis Grant. This film and other excellent shorts are available at nfb.ca. I must also thank my good friend Don Julien, CEO of the Confederation of Mainland Mi'kmaq, who kindly arranged for Mi'kmaw Elders and educators from the Mi'kmawey Debert Cultural Centre to review Maq's story and ensure its accuracy.

And, as always, thanks to Miriam.

–JBB
Halifax, Nova Scotia

June 1, 2019
Anniversary of the original National Child Day
(but celebrated on November 20 since 1993)

# INDEX